The Truth under Lock and Key?

The Truth under Lock and Key?

Jesus and the Dead Sea Scrolls

KLAUS BERGER

Translated by James S. Currie

Westminster John Knox Press
Louisville, Kentucky

Translated from *Qumran und Jesus: Wahrheit unter Verschluss?* © Quell Verlag, Stuttgart 1993

Book and cover design by Drew Stevens

First edition

Published by Westminster John Knox Press
Louisville, Kentucky

This book is printed on acid-free paper that meets the American National Standards Institute Z39.48 standard. ∞

PRINTED IN THE UNITED STATES OF AMERICA

95 96 97 98 99 00 01 02 03 04 — 10 9 8 7 6 5 4 3 2 1

Library of Congress Cataloging-in-Publication Data

Berger, Klaus, date.
    [Qumran und Jesus. English]
    The truth under lock and key? Jesus and the Dead Sea scrolls / Klaus Berger. — 1st ed.
        p.   cm.
    ISBN 0-664-25547-7 (alk. paper)
    1. Dead Sea scrolls—Criticism, interpretation, etc. 2. Dead Sea scrolls—Relation to the New Testament. I. Title.
BM487.B4613   1995
296.1'55—dc20   94-33665

For Christiane

Contents

Abbreviations

The texts from Qumran (except for the *Damascus Rule*) are so abbreviated that the number of the cave, that is, the place of discovery, is mentioned first with an Arabic number, then the letter "Q" always follows, then an abbreviation for the more precise title.

B.C.E.	Before the Common Era (=B.C.)
CD	*Damascus Rule* from the Cairo Genizah and Cave 1
C.E.	Common Era (=A.D.)
1QapGen	*Genesis Apocryphon*
1QH	*Thanksgiving Hymns*
1QpHab	*Pesher* (commentary) *on Habakkuk*
1QM	*War Rule*
1QS	*Community Rule*
1QSa	*Messianic Rule*
1QSb	*The Blessings*
1Q 27	*Book of Mysteries*
4QFlor	Florilegium (collection of quotations)
4QM	*War Scroll* from Cave 4
4QMMT	*Miqsat Ma'aseh Torah*
4QpPs37	*Midrash* (commentary) *on Psalm 37*
11QMelch	*Melchizedek* document
11QT	*Temple Scroll*
Vermes	Geza Vermes, *The Dead Sea Scrolls in English,* 3d ed., 1987

Part 1

Qumran and the
Mysterious Scrolls

Introduction
The Thriller

It is an unrivaled success. No other book on a religious topic has had such a wide-ranging impact in decades. Yet at the same time the verdict of specialists in the field is unanimously scathing.

I am referring to *The Dead Sea Scrolls Deception,* by Michael Baigent and Richard Leigh (New York: Summit Books, 1992). A second book pursues the same track: *The Dead Sea Scrolls Uncovered,* by Robert Eisenman and Michael Wise (Rockport, Mass.: Element Books, 1992), which offers fifty previously unpublished key texts from Qumran.

Both books are filled with the theories and ideas of Robert Eisenman. Furthermore, neither book has anything to do with Jesus. But the name of Jesus and the scent of a story that resolves a mystery combine for a bestseller.

Today if, like a teller of fairy tales, you wanted to tell a most exciting story suitable for helping ten- to fourteen-year-olds get through a rainy day at school, you would need the following ingredients: a conspiracy; a secret society; an anonymous international command center that always remains in the fog of mystery; the CIA; the Inquisition (which today would be secret, but thereby all the more exciting); hidden passageways in which something disappears; secret graves; falsified documents (suspicious enough!); cryptic documents, the codes of which must be cracked; a few rogues; some bright, honorable, lonely men with the courage for truth; two mysterious murders; and finally, a shady double agent who at some point became turned around, and yet was not turned around at all. The only thing lacking is a bit of sex, but unfortunately that must be omitted out of deference to the souls of innocent children. Thus the story remains a clean one.

Baigent and Leigh weave these requirements together into a thriller that takes place in two different times: in primitive Christianity and as a modern conspiracy surrounding the find at Qumran. The conspiracy is instigated by the international committee of editors of the Qumran texts, the secret group is the Ecole Biblique in Jerusalem; the command center is the Vatican; the CIA enters on cue; the Inquisition is conducted by Cardinal Ratzinger; the secret passageways are found in the Vatican, the mysterious graves in Qumran; the scrolls are presented as documents which, however, are falsified by the Inquisition. To be deciphered is the commentary on Habakkuk from Cave 1 in Qumran, and it is thus determined that James and Paul are meant. The rogues are, above all, the Dominican fathers Roland de Vaux and J. T. Milik. The lonely men with the courage for truth are played by John Allegro (his widow fed the authors third-class scholarly gossip) and a certain Robert Eisenman. Victims of the mysterious murders, carried out in the name of a syndicate of priests that collaborates with the occupiers, are Stephen and James. Finally unmasked as the double agent—this is the climax—is the apostle Paul. Understandably, he is the most despised figure in the whole story.

Obviously, all of this is neither intended seriously nor is it to be taken seriously. (One can imagine how the authors laughed up their sleeves while deciding what to say in the manuscript.) Nevertheless, the subtitle reads: "The Qumran Scrolls and the Truth about Early Christianity." Even that could be understood in the sense of an exciting thriller: "The Truth about John X." The only problem is that the matter at hand is not a mystery thriller.

When such a book is presented as a scholarly work, and, in addition, appears in the course of an antichurch wave, the exciting story has multiple effects on various levels. One not only reads it for conversation; one also experiences many things about a closed and unknown world: the Qumran find and the history of early Christianity. But above all, there is a possibility of applying the classic moral of mystery thrillers—which makes sharp distinctions between good and evil, rogues and heroes—to an unloved institution for which many have long wanted an exposure: the church, and, in this case, the Catholic Church. The multiple results work according to the principle that somehow there must be something to it, particularly because the publication of the Qumran texts was in fact inexplicably delayed.

With their spacious, bureaucratic administrative centers, Lutheran state churches are obviously far less suited for the structure of mystery thrillers than the "Vatican," which is surrounded with secrecy. Thus M. Merz reaches this conclusion in a review of the book: "With its historic dungeons the stronghold of men in Rome is excellently suited for such material. From a criminological point of view, on the other hand, a Lutheran church that is composed of synods is simply boring. Therefore, the logical consequence of the great interest in this book for Rome can only be: Do not change anything in the system! Successful sales refute the prose of journalists, the church may be dismissed as a historical error. It still shackles minds, entices the intellect, fills the coffers of publishers" (*Die Zeit,* August 28, 1992).

Precisely in this sense, the book has—albeit contrary to its declared intent—stimulated a large public interest in the Qumran finds and the history of primitive Christianity. What no fiery sermon, no courageous Christian resistance fighter, and no heroic nun could do, this book has done. The longing of every pastor and teacher of religion is now within reach: Many people have a burning interest in the beginnings of Christianity.

This interest must be addressed in a serious way. Thus, this book depicts the current situation of research and the reception of the Qumran finds, addresses questions that are raised regarding the history of primitive Christianity, and finally, treats the large and important topic of the close internal relationship between the Qumran texts and early Christianity.

Chapter 1
The Qumran Discoveries Today

The First Scandal

There was and is a full-fledged and robust scandal: By 1992, 45 years after the discovery of the scrolls at Qumran in 1947, a large portion (about 20 percent) of the Qumran find still had not been published. Only recently, in a roundabout way, an edition of numerous, heretofore unpublished texts reached my desk—an edition that came about only with extreme pressure from the international public and that appears to have no legal copyright protection. In 1979 I had to provide a new translation of and commentary on the book of *Jubilees*, one of the postcanonical writings of Judaism to which extensive references exist in the Qumran materials. At two-month intervals I turned three times to J. T. Milik (in Paris), the temporary "custodian" of the remaining Qumran texts, requesting collegial assistance. To this day I have received no response. And one has the impression that such is the case for all who do not belong to the inner circle of "keepers of the grail." The keepers are literally sitting on their fragments, from which only death will part them.

It is also true that misfortune has come to the most important editors: They became alcoholics or lost their minds, left their monastic orders, fell out with their (Catholic) church, or married (despite being priests). Toward the end of his life, one wrote a book in which he traced early Christianity back to poisonous mushrooms. Almost all these persons were and are cursed with scholarly sterility. No, it was not the Vatican Inquisition that hindered them, but a spirit of research that had become morbid, an aristocratic lethargy (and arrogance).

Nevertheless, soon all the texts will be published. The time when they were treated privately like samizdat literature is now past. Indeed, the Bible says that the last scandals will be greater than the first ones.

The Second Scandal

Approximately 80 percent of the preserved texts from Qumran have long since been published. They are available in either good or excellent translations. In addition to the translation of Geza Vermes, already mentioned, the reader might consult the following:

Theodor H. Gaster, *The Dead Sea Scriptures in English Translation,* 3d ed. (Garden City, N.Y.: Doubleday & Co., Anchor Books, 1976).

James S. Charlesworth et al., eds., *The Dead Sea Scrolls,* vol. 1: *Rules: Rule of the Community and Related Documents* (Tübingen: J.C.B. Mohr [Paul Siebeck]/Louisville, Ky.: Westminster John Knox Press, 1994); and vol. 2: *Rules: Damascus Document, War Scroll, and Related Documents* (forthcoming in 1995). (These volumes, to be followed by others, present the Hebrew, Aramaic, and Greek texts with English translations and annotations.)

The scandal is that these unique documents have not been compared to the New Testament in any thorough and systematic way. Occasionally in a very good seminar paper one finds a citation from these texts, but no one knows for sure what one is to do with them. And in sermons or pastoral work, it seems that one has never heard that these texts even exist. Scholarly commentaries on the New Testament include references to Qumran texts, though in the footnotes and always with other material. But who has the time to look them up? There has never been a broader theological interest in the materials.

One thing is certainly clear: Whether one dates these writings in the first century before Christ or after Christ, they are in any case the only received original texts from the time period that one can call the time of Jesus. By comparison, the oldest preserved Gospel fragments on papyrus are dated around 120 C.E.

That there was no theological interest in these texts can be attributed not only to the demanding schedules of pastors but also to the dominant mentality in the past few decades, especially in Germany, according to which one always felt compelled to dismiss the early Christian message somehow as one of "Jewish self-righteousness and works of piety." One always knew beforehand what the result would be. Because of the needs of a deep Christian identity crisis, the peculiarity of the New Testament (especially of Jesus and Paul) was constantly expressed at the expense of Judaism. A good example of this mentality is the only comprehensive study of a theological problem from the Qumran texts: Herbert Braun's *Spätjüdisch-häretischer und frühchristlicher Radikalismus* (Late Jewish heretical and early Christian radicalism) (2 vols., Tübingen, 1957).

In a stereotypical fashion, Judaism could only be reproached for pride in performance. Then the intensification of the Jewish laws in the Qumran texts had to be seen virtually as a demonic alternative to Jesus' teaching of grace. Hence it was thought to be a worthless, literalistic faith. But Christians themselves now often enough have reason to acknowledge precisely that same small-mindedness and narrow legalism.

When will Christian preaching finally learn that Christianity does not live by distinguishing itself from Judaism? That the Old Testament belongs truly and completely to the canon of the Bible and that early Christianity is an intensification of certain Jewish themes and not their destruction or condescending conquest? That Jesus has something else in mind than differentiating himself from Moses? And that therefore the Judaism during the time of Jesus was not the dark background for the luminous message, but rather the larger family providing the context for early Christians?

But heretofore, teaching and preaching have been otherwise. And thus an image of Jesus and of early Christianity arose that must disintegrate when it is now discovered that Jesus was a Jew, stood in the middle of the Judaism of his day, and participated in it—as did Paul; and furthermore, that Jesus was truly a human being and, as the Son of God, not a supermundane heavenly being.

It is indeed true that depictions of Judaism at the time of Jesus and of the genuinely Jewish character of everything Christian in the first century comes to "late Christian" persons in a difficult religious situation: Knowledge of their own religion is arguably meager. Pastors and ministers have—without malicious intent—ignored the Jewish and, come to think of it, the religious-historical side of the Bible, and all Christians everywhere are plagued by intensive (especially moral) questions of identity. In part these questions are heightened still further by the emphasis on the "confessionally stipulated" sinfulness of all people. When Christians explain publicly that they would be ashamed "of such a religion" (because everything is sin and darkness), then a few simple references to Jewish analogies could cause that fragile house to collapse completely.

In a great many churches Jesus never truly became a human being. His divine majesty was too strongly emphasized—that is, his distance from human beings in general and, therefore, from people even of his own day. In contrast to human sinfulness, Jesus' holiness, exaltation, and heroism grew ever higher and higher until the distance was so great that he was inaccessible. What remained was Christianity as faith in things that cannot be holy enough; in things that are, in any case, completely different from what is normal.

Many think that the title "Son of God" means exactly this. Thus, with no more instruction than what is received in confirmation classes, most people can have this high-sounding view of

God's Son fixed in their minds (not their hearts). With time this inevitably leads to an explosive situation. This occurs when the presumed absoluteness of Jesus is relativized by proof that much, if not almost everything, in the message of Jesus and of Paul is simply Jewish.

The natural polar opposite to everything high-sounding is distrust.

The Third Scandal

The third scandal is more aggravating than the first two, but it presupposes them. It concerns the theses of Robert Eisenman, Michael Baigent, and Richard Leigh, as well as their enthusiastic public reception. This public success is in itself a peculiar and interesting problem. It sheds a harsh light on today's religious situation: Churches are no longer trusted. Thus, at all times people credit them with deception and manipulation, even regarding the use of sources having to do with the beginning of Christianity.

This loss of confidence has many causes: political entanglements in the East, unrealistic sexual morals, internal ecclesiastical feuds, a shortage of trustworthy figures, an absence of spirituality among preachers. But more than anything the overall instability and uncertainty of human beings themselves is reflected in the loss of trust in churches. It is no accident that this trust is collapsing at the same time that clear ideological oppositions are disappearing, for identifying an enemy served to stabilize one's own identity. Wherever they have disappeared (even for moral reasons: one isn't supposed to have enemies), people have become uncertain. It is indeed true that nothing worse can happen between human beings than to have trust destroyed.

Let us turn to the part of the scandals that has to do with scholarly arguments.

Chapter 2
The Questionable Theses
of Robert Eisenman

In their book *The Dead Sea Scrolls Deception,* journalists Baigent and Leigh quite often refer to the theses of Robert Eisenman, who in his own publications developed his peculiar view of primitive Christianity. Eisenman sees the issue in the following way: Primitive Christianity was a movement of "Zealots," that is, nationalistic Jews of the first century C.E. who were prepared for violent political subversion and for preliminary "terrorist" acts of violence in order to expel the Romans from Palestine. The Lord's brother James (or perhaps even Jesus himself) is the "teacher of righteousness" mentioned in the Qumran writings. The community of Qumran is identical with the primitive Christian community, and Paul is a secret agent of the Romans. Thus, primitive Christianity was filled with tensions and conflicts between Paul and James. James, the Lord's brother, was not only faithful to the Jewish law but also extremely militant, prepared to use force, and hostile to foreigners. Paul, however, is depicted by Eisenman as the destroyer of Judaism and an enemy of the law.

If these theses are called "questionable" here, it is on the basis of historical-critical research regarding the Bible and its environment. Regarding this basis, the following should be noted: The research that has been engaged in for about the past 200 years was not devised by leaders in the church but by scholars who, using precisely the same means that are used in all historical and literary studies, assumed a (ruthlessly) critical attitude toward their respective confessions and their own religious convictions. In the course of a lengthy discussion, many hypotheses were proposed and then again discarded. But in this discussion there was and there is a broadly established framework within which one can and may move. This framework is the "critical consensus"; whoever ventures beyond it bears the entire burden of proof. If such proofs are not engaged in with care and in such a way that they truly illuminate something that was previously unknown, then one can be charged with recklessness, carelessness, or questionableness.

No scholar of literature or history would ever claim to have ascertained the ultimate truth—that is not possible in any facet of human history (and the "truth" of which the Bible itself speaks refers to something other than that which scholars are able to discover; it refers to God himself). But in the discussion one may expect arguments that make something at least probable and plausible. If such arguments are not supplied with bold theses, the originator of such opinions finds himself or herself outside the circle of discussion. And that is precisely the case with the theses of R. Eisenman. Over and over again it can be shown that Eisenman pursues "wild" and half-scholarly "theories" that no one in the nineteenth century believed and that have been justifiably forgotten, so that they can appear today as something new. In his charmingly written book *The Quest of the Historical Jesus* (1906; Eng. trans. 1910), Albert Schweitzer presents all these naive attempts with scorn and irony.

Above all, one can observe that Eisenman repeatedly claims to have a very precise knowledge of things which, scientifically, cannot ever be known so exactly. The following countertheses, therefore, are intended, not to demonstrate that "the expert" is a better "exegete," but rather to ask again: How can Eisenman know with such precision what the sources, despite one's best intentions as an interpreter, do not warrant? Because that is so consistently the case throughout, at the end there remains the impression of an extremely improbable and very arbitrary construction.

Inherent in these theses are substantive questions from the history of primitive Christianity.

Paul as "God-Creator"?

Thesis: Paul is supposed to have been the first to equate Jesus with God; Jesus would never have permitted the worship of a human being. All miracles, the legends about his being born of a virgin, and the resurrection are inventions of Paul.

Against this thesis: In his letters Paul makes no mention of any miracles of Jesus, and the tradition of Jesus' conception by the Holy Spirit is found in Luke and Matthew, not in Paul. Paul himself says that he received the faith in Jesus' resurrection as tradition (1 Cor. 15:3–4: "For I delivered to you as of first importance what I also received, that Christ died . . . , that he was raised on the third day in accordance with the scriptures . . ."). And regarding Jesus' divinity, nowhere in Christianity is Jesus viewed as "a second God"; rather, God is made visible in him, he represents God in a unique way, he is God's authorized agent. In him we worship no one other than the one and only God. Why is Paul supposed to have invented all of this? Prior to Paul, the group around Stephen mentioned something similar. According to everything we know, this group appealed particularly to the authority of Jesus. Thus, Stephen sees Jesus standing beside the throne of God (Acts 7:56) as the Son of man in highest conceivable dignity.

Baigent and Leigh speak of Paul as the actual founder of the new Christian religion that was hostile to the law, and of Paul who sold Jesus as "God" as one sells "soap or pet food," thereby contending for a market share among the gods. This image is not only a resuscitated model from the nineteenth century, but it is filled with hatred and grotesque stupidity. For with all the passion of his heart, Paul understood himself to be a Jew. With great sadness and constant pain he mourns for his brothers, and full of melancholy he asks whether God has deserted his people (Rom. 9:1–6 and 11:1–3). Modern biblical scholarship has at long last rediscovered him as a Jew. For Paul, Christianity is nothing other than messianic Judaism.

But wherever hatred becomes so clearly visible as in Baigent and Leigh, the uneasy reader asks whether only the subject matter is at stake or whether there might not also be at times a mirror image: Who is really contending for a share of the market here? Who is really trying to surpass the deeds of rival deities? For it simply cannot escape anyone that their judgments about Paul (and therefore about the whole of Christianity, which he presumably founded) are historically indefensible. They will never be able to lay claim to foundational substance or scholarly method. It is on a par with the light novel *Kaffeesatz der wildesten antikirchlichen Aufklärung* (Coffee grounds of the wildest anti-ecclesiastical enlightenment), by B. Streithofen, which speculates with superficial theological knowledge.

Antipathy against Paul goes so far that one of the two cited Old Testament passages in which Paul found reference to the justification of the faithful, namely, Habakkuk 2:4, is interpreted as an "apocryphal" text, one "which is said to come from the middle of the seventh century B.C.E." It is then presented as a great revelation that from here Paul copied his teaching regarding faith. Only a fool would accept this. First of all, in virtually every German [and English] translation of the Bible it is noted in Romans 1:17 and Galatians 3:11 that Paul expressly quotes this text, and second, as a source for Paul's teaching there is also the story of Abraham's faith being reckoned as righteousness [Gen. 15:6; see Rom. 4:3]. And third, the prophet Habakkuk is not apocryphal but part of every Hebrew Bible. But, of course, this argument is aimed at rubbing out Paul, debasing him, even if it is at the cost of the prophet Habakkuk.

Paul as Collaborator with the Romans and as Double Agent?

According to Acts 7, Saul, later Paul, was present at the stoning of Stephen. Luke writes that he had "consented to his death." Baigent and Leigh are unable to discern in the biblical text a reason for the execution of Stephen.

Thesis: As a Zealot, which everyone in the primitive Christian community was, Stephen was stoned by Paul, the Roman agent serving the pro-Roman Jewish priesthood.

Against this thesis: Stephen is stoned because he revives Jesus' threatening word against the Temple and thereby is seen as defeatist (it is as if someone were to appear at the Vatican as a prophet and announce the imminent destruction of St. Peter's Church); and because, according to Acts 7:56, he claims to see God and, beside him, the Son of man—which had to be viewed as blasphemy because Moses had not even seen God once.

Thesis: Later Paul undergoes the appearance of a conversion to Christianity. As destroyer of the Jewish law, he thereby serves the Romans further as a secret agent. But the primitive community at Qumran sees through this and identifies Paul and his people as transgressors of the law. Conversely, Paul informs the church in Jerusalem that it proclaims a different Jesus (2 Cor. 11:3–4).

Against this thesis: Paul does not do away with the Torah; rather, for him the law is holy, righteous, and good; it is spiritual (Rom. 7:12, 14). And the idea that in 2 Corinthians 11:3–4 when Paul speaks of the preachers of the "different Jesus" he means to name the Jerusalem church is simply not in the text; only scattered researchers have conjectured that. In particular, the letter to the Romans, which our authors do not like to mention by name, reserves for the later Paul a fundamentally positive relationship to Judaism.

Qumran as Damascus?

According to Acts 9:3, Paul was approaching Damascus when he saw a light, fell to the ground, heard the voice of Jesus—and was converted. And according to Acts 9:19–20, in Damascus there were disciples with whom he stayed before he proclaimed Jesus as the Son of God "in the synagogues." That the well-known city of Damascus was the locale of this event has heretofore not been questioned, and there is still no reason to question it.

But among the texts found in Qumran there is the so-called *Damascus Rule* (since 1896 a copy of this text has been known from the Cairo Genizah, a depository for ancient scrolls in the synagogue there). Its name was derived from the fact that its authors, as the text says, are concerned with a community "of the new covenant in the land of Damascus." Thus in 6:5 of the *Damascus Rule* we read that they were "the converts of Israel who went out of the land of Judah to sojourn in the land of Damascus," and in 6:19 we read: ". . . according to the finding of the members of the New Covenant in the land of Damascus" (Vermes, 87). Now the *Damascus Rule* itself indicates how we are to understand the site: In 7:14–16 of the *Damascus Rule,* we find an extensive commentary on Amos 5:26–27. But this passage, according to the biblical text, says the following: As punishment for idol worship, Israel is exiled "beyond Damascus." The hinterlands of Damascus, according to Amos, are the place of exile for Israel.

In the *Damascus Rule* (7:14–16) this passage from Amos is taken up and incorporated into an application of the so-called Deuteronomic view of history, according to which in the situation of dispersion among the nations Israel will convert and then be redeemed. Damascus stands for exile, for the foreign country into which Jews are dispersed. In this country they convert, and thus arises the new covenant.

The passage from the *Damascus Rule* has also often been interpreted differently: The supporters of true worship emigrated voluntarily to the region of Damascus. But according to our interpretation "the land of Damascus" stands for the foreign regions of exile (similar to "Babylon" elsewhere). A precise determination of the location is not possible.

The name "Damascus" is thus either a reference to the specific, well-known city of Damascus or to be understood symbolically in a way that defies precise geographic identification. But there is nothing that demonstrates that it has anything to do with Qumran. For one thing above all others is not established: that the inhabitants of Qumran saw themselves as the community of the new covenant from the "country" of Damascus. In Qumran only one copy of the scroll was found, but no one knows its origin.

Conclusion: There is no reason to doubt the Pauline Damascus. There is equally no chance of locating reliably the Damascus of the *Damascus Rule.* That both are identical with Qumran is an entirely arbitrary assumption.

Paul as Opponent of Jesus?

Among the cliches of the nineteenth century is the idea of a presumably insuperable opposition between Jesus and Paul. Paul is almost always the one who is "not liked," and in particular he must endure all the attacks that are constantly intended for the church.

Thesis: Paul "betrayed" Jesus' command to fulfill every jot and tittle of the law (Matt. 5:17–19). As an agent of the Romans, he fought against the primitive community that was faithful to the law.

Against this thesis: Paul did not do away with the law. He says expressly that it is "holy" and "from God's Spirit." The Holy Spirit that is bestowed on Christians should now rather make it altogether possible to fulfill God's law (Rom. 8:3–4). Thus Paul is also able to say that love is the fulfillment of all the commandments of the law. To maintain that would be fully absurd if it did not depend precisely on the fulfillment of the law. And Paul himself did not do away with the Old Testament prescriptions having to do with ritual and atonement. To a certain extent they lost something of their function because Jesus' death brought the relationship with God into order. But that is something completely different from dismissing the law. The same is also true for all commandments regarding purification as well as for circumcision. By means of the filial relationship to God in the Holy Spirit, all Christians are so near to God that such proximity must not be supplemented by circumcision or purification commandments. Their consideration would indeed mean doubting the effect of the gift of the Spirit. However, in all its ethical and social regulations the law needs to be fulfilled by Christians. And now they have the strength (through God's Spirit) to be able to fulfill God's will.

Conclusion: The opposition between Jesus and Paul cannot rest on the notion that Paul did away with the law.

But might one possibly draw attention by wearing another old hat?

Jesus and the First Christians as Zealots?

The New Testament contains no suggestion whatsoever that Jesus or any authoritative persons of early Christianity (besides "Simon the Zealot" in Luke 6:15 and Acts 1:13, the origin of whose nickname we do not know) had been Zealots. Yet again and again since the nineteenth century, Jesus has been seen as a Zealot.

If we look at the representatives of this position, a very strong self-interest is evident. What is the interest of the scholars who like to see Jesus as a Zealot? Among them are combative socialists who make Jesus the forerunner of a violent class struggle. And there have also been, again and again, Jewish scholars who with such a thesis wish to explain primitive Christianity—which has always been incomprehensible to them—and to try to weaken the accusation by Christians that the Jews had murdered Jesus (which had an altogether calamitous history of influence) by suggesting that as the number-one terrorist enemy of the state, Jesus had been a particular thorn in the side of the Romans.

Since the nineteenth century, three texts have been repeatedly mentioned as supposedly demonstrating the fanaticism of Jesus: Jesus' actions against the money changers in the Temple (Mark 11:15), the equipping of the disciples with two swords (Luke 22:38), and the statement about Jesus' having come to bring a sword (Matt. 10:34).

Against this thesis the following can be said: Jesus' action against the traders in the Temple was not a military action but rather a messianic sign of religious character. With it the Messiah announces that the outer court may no longer be used for exchanging money (into Temple currency) and selling sacrifices, but that instead the Gentiles will worship him because in the last days, which are now dawning with Jesus, all nations will acknowledge the Lord of Israel. By his violent action, Jesus makes clear that the new era is no longer announced only with words but that God's sanctuary is purified from now on. By means of this sign Jesus provokes, as he does otherwise. But this action is a symbol of the real and not a fanatic rebellion: Jesus creates in the present a small portion of the future Temple reality. But this portion is still very modest: Here we have only a symbolic act—nothing more but also nothing less.

According to Luke 22:38 ("Look, Lord, here are two swords" and "It is enough"), either Jesus means that the disciples should not and need not arm themselves further, or in fact he grants permission for them to take two short swords on their dangerous journeys; the swords would be comparable to a spray carried by postal carriers to ward off dogs. At the most then, it was considered to be a defensive weapon, the use of which would be limited here by Jesus. It could certainly not be used to conduct a war.

Finally, when Jesus says, "I have not come to bring peace, but a sword" (Matt. 10:34; compare Luke 12:51, " . . . but rather division"), the immediate context illustrates how that is to be understood: as the division of natural, familiar ties when a part of the extended family acknowledges Jesus. One moves out and follows after Jesus. The sword is an image for the painful division of that which used to belong together.

Precisely in the context of this discussion, it is repeatedly observed (also by Baigent and Leigh) that in the face of Jesus' original message, the "Gospels" have been "falsified," reporting what is not truthful about Jesus.

Christian exegetical research since about 1830, particularly since the so-called *Tendenz* ("tendency") criticism of the Tübingen theologian Ferdinand Christian Baur, has been aware of such tendencies in the depiction of the evangelists themselves. In particular since the redaction criticism of the mid-1960s, scholars have discovered that the evangelists had certain theological and even political interests; that, for example, all of them are friendly toward Rome and exonerate Pilate in their portrayal, and in contrast lay blame on the Jewish masses and Judas.

In all likelihood Jesus' message, at least in its consequences, was not as friendly to Rome as it now appears on the basis of the Gospels. And the Revelation of John might have preserved better the original trajectory of Jesus' message in political terms than have other texts in the New Testament. But in this regard the standard for every judgment can only be, once again, all the sources of the first century C.E.

Based on the sources, and despite one's best intentions, one can at most make the following observations: The proclamation of the coming kingdom of God and/or of the Son of man also necessarily signified the end of all earthly rule. But the coming of this new era is nowhere attributed to violent actions by human beings. Rather, it is always and fundamentally a miraculous event that is brought about by God's activity (and that of God's angels). It was different with the Zealots.

In opposition to this, Baigent and Leigh maintain that primitive Christianity was "one of the manifestations of Judaic nationalism at the time—a body of militant individuals intent on upholding the Law, deposing the corrupt Sadducee priesthood of the Temple, . . . and driving the occupying Romans from the Holy Land" (194). As they see it, all Christians in the first century wanted to follow the law strictly. Everything else is unprovable or the opposite is true.

Conclusion: Jesus and many early Christian communities had apocalyptic tendencies; that is, they believed in the imminent end of every earthly rule. But they did not attempt to bring this about with violence or their own power. That distinguished them from the Zealots.

Jewish Groups as Zealots?

A wide variety of Jewish groups of the first century are wantonly lumped together as Zealots by Baigent and Leigh. Thus such groups as the Essenes, the inhabitants of Qumran, the apocalyp- ticists, and a radical wing of the Sadducees are treated as one.

But it is never explained whether the Therapeutae or the Es- senes, mentioned in the first-century Jewish writers Philo and Josephus and elsewhere, are the same as the groups discussed in the various texts from Qumran or only related to them. There are similarities and differences. But if one maintains that there is a relationship, it is not at all clear whether—and if so, how—the inhabitants of Qumran lived according to the writings of their library (and especially it is not clear which of the rules found among them they followed). And if any or all of these groups were "the" Essenes, they were by no means fanatics.

Apart from the question of how far the Qumran documents re- flect the actual conditions and beliefs of the inhabitants of the small settlement, there is not one that has a zealotic character in the whole of the old and new texts. That is also true for the so-called *War Scrolls* (1QM and 4QM). In a magic-ritual way, they depict a final battle in which, above all, angels will participate. However, all these elements are lacking in reports about Zealots, whom one must imagine as similar to modern terrorists or guerrillas.

It can actually be said that in the first century c.e. there existed in Judaism a variety of religious groups that as a whole distin- guished themselves by a certain faithfulness to the law. But it is quite impossible to attribute to all of them a terrorist character and to make them Zealots. The first century is not so impenetra- ble that, like cats at night, all groups alike seem gray.

For example, almost all apocalyptic groups characteristically required nonviolence and relied on God's monopoly on force. All Christians and the Essenes, according to Philo, also belonged to such representatives of nonviolence. This means that in the first century c.e. the imminent end of the world was considered quite likely (and they were thus "apocalypticists"), and in spite of that, or precisely because of that, any use of violence in the present was renounced. That is consistent. The association of apocalypticism with the renunciation of violence in early Christian writings can- not therefore be seen as subsequent falsification. Ninety percent of all Jewish apocalypticists of that time thought the same way.

The Inhabitants of Qumran
as a Primitive Christian Community?

In Acts 24:5 we read regarding Paul that he is the leader of "the sect of the Nazarenes." This is the only place in the New Testament that the word refers to a group. However, it is not a reference to the primitive church but rather to Paul and his congregation or congregations. Many hypotheses have been offered as to the precise meaning of the expression.

According to Baigent and Leigh, the phrase "keepers of the covenant" (Hebrew: *noṣrei haberit*) is supposed to have stood behind the obscure designation of the early Christians as Nazarenes (Greek: Nazoreans). Baigent and Leigh state [citing Eisenman] that it is contained in the Habakkuk commentary, but in fact it is not. One can simply see that in the old and new Qumran texts the terms "covenant" and "entry into covenant" are often mentioned.

If the expression "keepers of the covenant" is found in the Qumran texts, a group designation could be derived from this expression. It would remain to be demonstrated that the expression referred only to "the community" of Qumran and was used only there. For the expression is very general, just as references to covenant were in the Judaism of that time.

To use this flimsy hypothesis as the basis for the assumption that the inhabitants of Qumran were "the" primitive church requires simply too much faith without enough evidence. Moreover, how is it possible to explain and eradicate everything the New Testament reports about the early Jerusalem groups of Christians, the circle around the twelve disciples, the "Hebrews" and the "Hellenists," and the fact that the latter two groups were obviously structured like synagogue communities?

James the Brother of Jesus
as the "Teacher of Righteousness"?

To say that the term "the Righteous One," as Stephen refers to Jesus in Acts 7:52, originated specifically and uniquely from the vocabulary of the Qumran writings is simply not true; for example, the Messiah is so identified in the book of *Enoch* that came from Ethiopia (*1 Enoch* 38:2 and 53:6). Even a brief glance in a Bible commentary unearths these Jewish analogies from the second century before Christ. Apart from that, there are many examples, not simply in Qumran, of the non-Messianic use of "the righteous one." The "teacher of righteousness," a figure that is well known in several Qumran documents, is simply not identical with every person who is mentioned as "the righteous one."

It is as if, just because Jesus bears the title "the holy one," now every "holy one" is to be identified with Jesus.

Conclusion: According to later Christian texts, James the brother of Jesus bore the title "the righteous one." And according to Qumran texts there was a "teacher of righteousness," a righteous teacher. But the two must by no means be identical because in early Judaism there is hardly a term more frequently used than "the righteous one."

As a nickname, as in the case of James, the attribute "the righteous one" ["Justus"] is found three times in the New Testament alone: for Joseph Barsabbas in Acts 1:23, for Titus in Acts 18:7, and for a certain Jesus in Colossians 4:11. Are all these persons perhaps also identical with the "teacher of righteousness"? In fact, the title "the righteous one" and the nickname Justus are so widely used that no conclusions can be drawn from this regarding identity of persons.

Paul and James
as Mortal Enemies?

In their depiction of early Christian history, Eisenman and his journalistic emulators love to paint in black and white. Again and again the purpose is to portray some Christians as terrorists and others as destroyers of Judaism. The two are really incompatible. But that is obviously the desire of the authors: to show that early Christianity is in itself a bizarre impossibility. All important persons must have been, therefore, mortal enemies. But because none of this is found in the New Testament, one must presume what lies "behind it" and, cost what it may, construct an alternative.

Thus in Acts James is said to be characterized as a villain. He was the "legalistic" adversary of Paul. The Habakkuk commentary from Qumran depicts this mortal enmity in an encoded fashion. But nothing of this can be seen in the New Testament. At the Apostolic Council, James defends the mission to the Gentiles in a sympathetic speech. Thus, according to Acts 15:13–21, he says that the circumcision-free mission to the Gentiles is proper so that, as it is written, "the rest of men may seek the Lord, and all the Gentiles who are called by my [God's] name" (v. 17).

According to Baigent and Leigh, Paul stands for faith and James for the law. But how does this scarcely passable distortion stand with regard to Paul's words that the whole purpose of Jesus' coming was to enable human beings to fulfill the law (Rom. 8:4: "in order that the just requirement of the law might be fulfilled in us, who walk not according to the flesh but according to the Spirit"), and that circumcision or noncircumcision counts for nothing, only the keeping of God's commandments (1 Cor. 7:19)?

On the other side, without protest James agrees with Peter's speech according to which, by God's grace, everyone is saved who believes, and he continues Peter's speech in his own statements. Of course these speeches may not be considered "genuine," but the image painted of James at the time obviously allows this depiction.

When in Galatians 2:12 "people from James" reprimand Peter (not Paul!) for his freewheeling interpretation of the Jerusalem agreements, behind it, according to more recent research, stands James's concern for the security of his Jewish-Christian church in Jerusalem, on the one hand, and the wider church membership with Gentile Christians, on the other. Today James is seen as a wise, diplomatically reconciling preserver of the unity of the Christian movement between radical forces, a role which cost him his life. His martyrdom thus becomes understandable only in this context.

Eisenman and his colleagues place particular emphasis on

the contention that the false prophet in the Habakkuk commentary from Qumran is identical with Paul. The argument is this: According to the Habakkuk commentary, the false prophet was the adversary of the Teacher of Righteousness. If the Teacher of Righteousness is James and Paul is his opponent, then it must follow that Paul is the false prophet. Ostensible proof: In 2 Corinthians 11:31 Paul says: "God . . . knows that I do not lie," and in 1 Timothy 2:7 the (presumably) same Paul (that scholars do not consider this letter Pauline is withheld from the readers) says, "I am telling the truth, I am not lying." These two examples are enough to observe that Paul demonstrates an almost compulsive desire to vindicate himself against the charge of deceit, and this proves that he is the false prophet. So simplistic is the argument.

Thesis: After James's death, which Paul plotted, Paul was then seized by the Romans in the Temple for appearance sake, in order to cover up his participation in the murder. As thanks for his secret services, he received a new identity. The "open" conclusion of Acts explains this.

Against this thesis: The murder plot is fantasy. That Acts ends not with the martyrdom of Paul but with his arrival in Rome can only give rise to wild speculation for one who demands that Luke must have known what we know and should have portrayed what we demand. Luke does not present full biographies of the apostles (even of the martyrdom of Peter he says nothing) but rather depicts the path of the gospel. And when in Acts 1:8 we read that the gospel will extend to the end of the earth, Rome would have been the end, at least as seen from the eastern part of the empire. For Luke, the disobedience of the Jews and the openness of the Gentiles are the pervasive theme on this path. The concluding verses of this book reflect this, for Paul appeals to the Jews not to compete with their fathers in stubbornness, and as a contrast to that he mentions the readiness of the Gentiles to listen (Acts 28:28). From that closing note (Acts 28:31) is to be understood that Paul preached without hindrance: namely, without hindrance in contrast to that which he experienced more often among a portion of his Jewish audience. However, this Jewish opposition to Paul was, again and again, the justification for turning to the Gentiles.

In addition, Baigent and Leigh make much use of the later legendary portrayals of James in the so-called Pseudo-Clementines, a group of writings from the fourth century. In these texts Paul is indeed accepted as an "enemy" of Jewish Christians. For the groups that stand behind these texts the intention was to establish a polemical biographical depiction of Paul that reduced the significance Paul had for the larger church. What is found here about the roles of Paul is taken literally by Baigent and Leigh and interpreted as historical fact. That, however, is not possible. The tendency and origin of these documents are still to be explained.

New Testament Texts in Qumran?

In Cave 7 of Qumran two Greek fragments, among others, were found. They contain only a few letters. It has been assumed that they originated from Mark's Gospel and 1 Timothy. We have scanty scraps of papyrus on which 12 or 14 letters appear on each of three or four lines. Without doubt, thousands of Greek texts can be quoted that (with even more uncertain line lengths) contain this combination of letters. In addition to this uncertainty is the fact that the champions of the hypothesis that these are Christian texts must also accept two scribal errors among these few letters.

Thus this thesis has to be rejected as ultimately unprovable. The goal of determining an original date of New Testament texts and at the same time of ignoring critical scholarship that dates 1 Timothy long after Paul (but Qumran was destroyed about 70 C.E.) can be pursued more convincingly in other ways. It is generally questionable what the relationship is between the Greek fragments from Cave 7 and the rest of the texts.

Chapter 3
Who Were the People of Qumran?

The Old Consensus

Older attempts to shed light on the question of the identity of the inhabitants of Qumran were often characterized by little patience and an explicit tendency to make hasty equations and easy identifications. That means that the possessors of the Qumran texts were quickly identified with one of the other groups that was already well known, and the individual figures mentioned in them were equated with known persons of prominence from the first century C.E. It would be as if in the year 2900 C.E. someone were excavating in Weimar and believed every old scrap of paper to be a relic of Goethe because the only thing known about Weimar was that Goethe lived there. Some have claimed to have resolved the mystery of the scrolls by that kind of equation. Even the most recent interpretations by Eisenman, Baigent, and Leigh fall worthily into this series of attempts. The following explanations characterize the older consensus.

Some simply identified the Qumran inhabitants with the Essenes or the Therapeutae, who were known from other accounts. Well-known differences were swept under the rug. Thus some speak distantly of the Qumran Essenes.

Some equated the people of Qumran with the followers of John the Baptist or even with the primitive Christian church.

And some, without much thought, spoke of Qumran "sects" and thereby presupposed both schism (separation) and heresy (false teaching) in comparison to contemporary Judaism. The point of orientation was often the old theory of Adolf Hilgenfeld

(1823–1907) that in Judaism there was a so-called "apocalyptic conventicle." Because such groups were known in the church history of Württemberg, it was believed that apocalyptic ideas in Judaism could also be found in conventicles and sectlike organizations.

Every sect always presupposes an existing "orthodoxy" against which it is contrasted. For a very long time this orthodoxy was thought to have been found in early Pharisaic Judaism, a hypothesis that was strengthened and took hold in the rich compilation by H. Strack and P. Billerbeck, *Kommentar zum Neuen Testament aus Talmud und Midrasch* (Commentary on the New Testament from Talmud and Midrash).

But this ostensible opposition to a contemporary early rabbinical orthodoxy as well as the orthodoxy itself are pure fiction for the first century A.D. This means that the thesis of the "sect" is nothing more than the result of a comparison from a modern perspective. Moreover, the group from Qumran that was supposedly hermetically cut off could be distinguished from the Christianity that was supposedly always open to the world because in this comparison Christianity naturally did not appear to be a sect.

But what is most pernicious about the common catchword "sect" is undoubtedly that contemporary Judaism could be seen as completely oriented to the Old Testament and that a sect mentality could be held responsible for the intensive use, which is clearly evident, of extra-canonical religious writings. That is to say that one's own biblicism is introduced and the group from Qumran fares poorly vis-à-vis Jesus and Paul (as if the New Testament itself had not been a production of extra-canonical religious writings until the church declared it to be canonical).

A further attempted explanation is the discussion of the "Qumran community," by which here again central European (ideal) notions were introduced into the texts. In that regard the *mebaqqer* (curator) of the Qumran texts quickly becomes a "bishop" and as such is also then able to get into German bishops' festschrifts (e.g., the festschrift for Cardinal J. Frings).

Finally, the Qumran people are discussed as a "monastic community," with celibacy and strict monastic rules. Graves of women and children, which have also been found in Qumran, must somehow then be otherwise explained. In 4Q 502 a marriage liturgy has been discovered, and the new wisdom texts from Qumran obviously deal with husband and wife, father and mother. One must also overlook the fact that only about 400 years later did monastic societies with "common life" appear for the first time in all of our culture.

But above all, all the documents that were discovered in the caves are identified, in terms of their content, with the perspective of the inhabitants in a remarkable and completely inexplicable fiction. It is done in the framework of a theological history of development that can only be assumed from a point of view that makes me responsible for the content of all the writings in my library. Precisely the many new texts from Cave 4, which are now accessible through the publication of Eisenman and Wise, make it completely impossible, by their abundance and internal diversity, to understand them as a unique sectarian theology. They range from a poem of praise to Alexander Jannaeus to mystical texts about the throne chariot, from astrological texts about amulets against evil spirits to specific regulations for the man who "loves his bodily discharges," whatever that may be.

Finally, one also has to establish here whether the texts from Qumran may be the stored Temple library from Jerusalem. One wants to know, and as usual, one must know this quite precisely.

Not unimportant for these identifications is also the effort to identify the "teacher of righteousness" ("righteous teacher") in the Habakkuk commentary historically with other prominent persons. Thus in a smattering of legends he is made into the founder of the entire "sect" of Qumran. He becomes the composer of the hymns of Qumran (but the opponents of the "teacher" in the texts that mention him are not called "false prophets" as in 1QH 4:16). He becomes the author of the "letter" on the "justification by works" (4QMMT) and many other writings. In reality, this figure appears only in the *Damascus Rule* (CD) and the Habakkuk commentary (1QpHab) and not in the new texts.

However, according to our cultural thought patterns, especially as inherited from the nineteenth century, a monastery cannot come about without a founder and a sect especially cannot be established without a founding figure. One finally explains the Teacher of Righteousness as identical with John the Baptist or (see above) with James the brother of Jesus—again only the final steps in the list of hasty, impatient equations.

Again and again it is the same thought process: One cannot let the mysterious remain unresolved, but rather one lets one's thoughts run away with other well-known figures because one does not have the patience to leave something in semidarkness. Finally, this goes on until one can no longer assume any distinction between primitive church, Zealots, apocalypticists, and Essenes. It becomes clear that in a certain sense the new literary scandals are the continuation of a not completely uncommon method of "arranging" in general the texts found in Qumran. At the moment the exclusive identifications are particularly disturbing.

As a final recourse in questions of dating one enlists the aid of paleography (an attempt to date the Qumran texts on the basis of the handwriting) or determination by carbon-40 tests. In my view these efforts fail because of the short length of time that is involved (from the middle of the second century B.C.E. to the last third of the first century C.E.). It has been justifiably noted that the writing style says nothing about how long a scroll was in use.

All datings of the time of origin of the Qumran texts are so far extremely questionable. But all the same they contain nothing about Christianity. The archaeological discoveries at Qumran that require inspection have contributed nothing to theological questions.

A More Cautious Way

In order not to succumb to hasty false conclusions, one should, first of all, not simply treat as of equal significance information about various groups in ancient Judaism that resided in the "wilderness"—trying to live in a way pleasing to God—and one should not relate all important information to all these people. For there are at least six different groups to be distinguished:

John the Baptist (and followers), according to Mark 1:3, 4 ("the voice of one crying in the wilderness . . . John the baptizer appeared in the wilderness"). He baptizes in a place where the Jordan River flows through a desert region.

People who do penance in the desert and live there with the animals, eat plants, and reject the goods of civilization (including personal hygiene); thus Nebuchadnezzar according to Daniel (Septuagint) 4:33a and 33b. The point is prayer for one's sins and also for a vision.

Essenes, according to Pliny, *Natural History* 5.73: Essenes are "companions of the palm trees below which was the city of En-gedi."

Disciples of prophets mentioned in the *Ascension of Isaiah* (2:8–11), a Jewish document of the first century B.C.E. in which relationships of the first century C.E. are read into the time of Isaiah: "And there also there was great iniquity; and he [Isaiah] withdrew from Bethlehem and dwelt on a mountain in a desert place. And Micah the prophet, and the aged Ananias, and Joel, and Habakkuk, and Josab his son, and many of the faithful who believed in the ascension into heaven, withdrew and dwelt on the mountain. All of them were clothed in sackcloth, and all of them were prophets; they had nothing with them, but were destitute, and they all lamented bitterly over the going astray of Israel. And they had nothing to eat except wild herbs (which) they gathered from the mountains" (tr. M. A. Knibb, in James H. Charlesworth, ed., *The Old Testament Pseudepigrapha,* vol. 1; Garden City, N.Y.: Doubleday & Co., 1983).

Maccabeans and Judas Maccabeus according to 2 Maccabees 5:27: "But Judas Maccabeus, with about nine others, got away to the wilderness, and kept himself and his companions alive in the mountains as wild animals do; they continued to live on what grew wild, so that they might not share in the defilement."

Inhabitants of Qumran: That the people of Qumran themselves understood themselves as being "in the wilderness" could reflect their interest in the commentary on the Psalms in which the subject matter is "those who will return from the wilderness" (4QpPs 37 3.1). The *Community Rule* (1QS 8:12–14; 9:19f.) uses, as does Mark 1:3, the quotation from Isaiah 40:3 concerning the voice of one crying in the wilderness. Because the quotation in Isaiah 40:3 comes from the Old Testament does not mean that all people who appeal to it are identical.

It is obvious then that there were various groups with distinctive characteristics that withdrew from the hellenized city life seeking renewal in the uncultivated countryside. If the alternative to life in the city and the return to "paternal customs" for wealthy Romans of the time consisted in living on a country estate in a country house (villa), the withdrawal from the cities in Palestine into the wilderness is substantially more burdensome and is depicted as an ascetic journey. But as with the Romans, it is a more universal custom, a kind of fashion, so to speak, of seeking a pleasant connection with the idealized ancient time outside the city. In Jesus we find both: a devotion to the cities but also words of judgment about the cities, on the one hand, and prayer, transfiguration, and accounts of feedings in desolate places, on the other. The word "desert" awakens quite false associations.

Conclusion: In Judaism there are very diverse groups that seek a new beginning in the wilderness. They are not identical.

Let us now take the next steps on the "more cautious" way.

Even groups that are generally included under the catchword "Essenes" are not at all identical. And to speak legitimately of Qumran Essenes can be disputed, for it would mean understanding Essenes in a very broad sense. Among others, Philo and Josephus (Greek-speaking Jews of the first century C.E.) speak of Essenes, but their accounts are anything but uniform. For example, while, according to Josephus, the Essenes were a tightly organized ascetic group that lived with (nominal) common ownership and were for the most celibate, having separated themselves from the Sanctuary, according to Philo they lived rather in the cities and villages of Palestine, dispersed among them. Once again, the Therapeutae, whom Philo describes in his writing *On the Contemplative Life,* are to be distinguished from the others.

Conclusion: In the Judaism of that day there were various reform groups that aspired to a stricter and purer life in a certain social framework. From that perspective Christians also belonged among these reformers. It is impossible to combine all these groups into one sect. It would be as if one considered all advocates of "organic foods" or vegetarianism in our century to be a uniform sect with communistic structures.

Regarding the absence of a "sect structure" in the Qumran group, several observations can be made on the basis of the book of *Jubilees. Jubilees* is a retelling of the biblical story from the creation of the world to the flight from Egypt. It originated at the latest in the middle of the second century B.C.E. Nine copies of it were found in Qumran. In its particular statements, the *Damascus Rule* is thought to be, in part, a kind of "exposition" of its theology. This can be shown especially in the rules for the Sabbath.

With my commentary on the book of *Jubilees,* I was able to demonstrate (and this is also undisputed in the research) that this text presupposes no "sect structure" at all nor does it have that as a goal. Rather, it is directed at all of Israel and strives for its complete renewal. *Jubilees* was not written for a "sect." And as for the *Damascus Rule,* it has already been made clear that the word "Damascus" is a symbolic locution. Even if a circle of authors was involved, that circle thought of itself as the core of Israel desiring reform and not as a sect. In all likelihood the *Rule* is aimed at Diaspora Jews ("in the country of Damascus") because they were awaiting renewal. The early Christians also had a similar self-understanding as the renewed core of Israel. Even if the authorship could be localized, personally and geographically, by no means does all this indicate an exclusive identity with the group at Qumran.

The Inhabitants of Qumran

From what has been said so far, we may conclude the following: The critical question is how much about the group of residents of this small settlement may be known from the documents found in the caves at Qumran. It appears impossible that all the documents found there were also intended for this community as obligatory norms. For that reason a conclusion, in the sense of a word-for-word identification, is barred. If that cannot be the case, there remains only the question of the basic interest people may have had in the collection of these documents.

Consider a comparison: From the books owned by a New Testament scholar today, one would not be able to determine the scholar's lifestyle; one could only try to some extent to determine his or her interests.

Now without doubt there are places in the texts that one may assume more closely reflect concrete daily life than other places. The interest of the inhabitants of Qumran will, therefore, have been concrete in varying degrees in relation to the particular document and passages. What we would characterize as literary "loftiness" or (carefully stated) "quality" is a simple and easily manipulated criterion. That is to say, financial accounts and texts of treaties are very clearly tied to historical reality and are clearly linked to it, whereas benedictions, hymns, depictions of heaven and the heavenly Jerusalem, and adaptations of biblical texts might have claimed a higher degree of general acceptance. It should be noted that these are "suspicious" criteria that must be tested in each case.

If this graduated specificity of interest can be generally agreed upon as a basis for criteria of "approximation of life" in documents, then for the texts from Qumran it could mean the following: In those texts that venture farthest in specifying everyday life, one may first assume that they were literally applicable to the residents of Qumran. Enumerated in a series that begins with the most specific, that would include precise calculations of the calendar (based on the sun calendar accepted there), astrological information, purity casuistry, and rules concerning eating together at meals. Everything is applicable as long as no texts appear that substantively compete with or diverge from those held by the same owners.

If one accepts that, then one may say, for example, that in all likelihood casuistic texts such as 1QS (the *Community Rule*) would support conjectures regarding customs that were actually practiced here.

Texts with veiled allusions to persons of the more recent past are a special case. Belonging to that group are the texts that mention "the righteous teacher," that is, only the *Damascus Rule* (CD) and the commentary on Habakkuk (1QpHab). From the same period the puzzling (and mysteriously named) figure of Taxo in the *Testament of Moses*—which was not found in Qumran—is comparable. Whoever collected such texts would presumably have known the true identity of the person being named. Of course nothing is said about the actual significance or even the function of the founder of a "community."

Apart from these earlier, marginal documents, however, one must inquire into the more general interest that is documented in the numerous texts from Qumran. Such an interest can only be reconstructed in the Qumran texts by asking about the common denominator of these writings. We find that the particular interest of these people appears less in the Old Testament writings than in the later texts that are preserved here. For, as we know from authors that can be dated in this period (Philo, New Testament), the Old Testament writings were, to a great extent, the property of everyone and therefore permit fewer specific conclusions.

Second, why were these people collecting scrolls at all, and some with several copies? The texts that were newly composed at the time provide the answer themselves: The Palestinian Judaism of that day was, to a very high degree, seeking a national and religious identity and increasingly found it in the "writings of the fathers" and other pseudepigraphic texts. Above all, in these centuries Judaism became a religion of the written word, a book religion, and the canon was closed in this time period. Again and again in the documents themselves we find references to writings of the fathers, statements and writings of Enoch, Abraham, and Seth, to "testaments" of the patriarchs, and similar references. And it is in this period that systematic beginnings are made in the interpretation of texts that will soon be defined as the canon and that Christians will then call the Old Testament. Such systematic interpretation is found in the first century B.C.E. to a previously completely unknown degree; it is found in Philo of Alexandria, in the Qumran texts, and in the New Testament.

Conclusion: Whoever sought a renewal of Judaism in the Judaism of the first century C.E. did so on the basis of ancient or supposedly ancient writings. And that was certainly the case not only in Qumran. Even far beyond Judaism there was an international phenomenon of national resistance against a uniform Hellenistic culture.

For the persons responsible for the collection of the texts found at Qumran, there is the following "common denominator": They understood Hebrew and Aramaic (the role of the Greek fragments in Cave 7 is unclear) and spent a relatively large amount of time reading (multiple copies of many texts). Their life clearly bore a religious stamp, and not in the sense of immersing themselves in the commandments of the Torah but in the sense of definition and specificity. They were interested in the concrete exercise of their faith. Hellenization in the sense of a leveling with the Gentile lifestyle cannot be discerned. Rather, the popularity of the book of *Jubilees* and the reverence for the Sabbath clearly point to a tendency against all hellenization. In light of this interest the existence of the poem of praise to King Jonathan (Alexander Jannaeus?) in 4Q 448 can also be understood. It reveals that the inhabitants of Qumran in any case joined with the Maccabees in their anti-Hellenistic interest. This is the least common denominator.

Pointing to that also is the tendency toward calendar calculations, a tendency that is strongly prominent in the newly published texts. I am certainly not able to evaluate this interest as particularly "priestly," but I do see in it an emphasis on the Sabbath, which in my view can be understood more as anti-Hellenistic. For the reactions of Gentile authors to Judaism show again and again that the Sabbath was *the* characteristic mark and identifying sign of Judaism.

The conception of purity plays an important role in these interests. Repeatedly one finds documents in which it is important. Even this is not a specifically priestly problem but rather one of religious identity in a minority situation because here priestly criteria are transferred to all members of the group. The selection of apocalyptic texts in Qumran demonstrates that by the preservation of ritual purity one also expected the presence of angels and, with that, survival in the coming end time. The place of "priestly" interests in many Qumran documents, therefore, arose from a widespread expectation at this time that the observance of priestly rules would have a kind of magical-sacramental effect toward the deliverance of the whole nation. Thus, the texts need not have been composed and used by Temple personnel; rather, the cultic interest served that national interest. According to these "cultic" texts, the magical-sacramental deliverance of Israel is the other side of the internal renewal by conversion. Everything in these texts aims at a comprehensive reestablishment of Israel. For this reason also the Hebrew documents predominate, because the use of Hebrew was an expression of the national and religious turning.

A fundamental opposition to the Temple in Jerusalem is not discernible in this perspective.

Furthermore, there is an interest in apocalyptic eschatology, but by itself this is not a defining characteristic.

The texts go on to show a pervasive interest in particular kinds of communal meetings (meals and "stipulations for exclusions").

However, that does not suggest a permanent *vita communis,* a monastic communal life. Rather, as Matthias Klinghardt has recently noted, the Qumran texts on community meals and community rules in general are similar to the rules for Hellenistic associations (including those governing Essene meals). If this analogy is valid (and in my view there can be no doubt that it is), then this means that the structure of the group at Qumran cannot be distinguished from the association-like structure of Jewish communities as it has been otherwise documented in the surrounding area. Like ancient religious associations, Christians also saw the center of their identity in their communal meals, which were observed, in part, as a remembrance of Jesus' last supper.

From what has been said, the following important corrections are submitted vis-à-vis the customary image of the inhabitants of the settlement at Qumran:

The residents of Qumran were not a special sect in the Judaism of the time with an exotic character. They document a religious life that is surely intensive, but in its way completely typical.

That also explains why the extra-canonical writings that we find here are also found elsewhere. They were read not simply in Qumran, nor did they originate here. To these writings belong especially the *Enoch* literature, the book of *Jubilees,* the analogies (already noted) to the literature of the testaments (particularly the *Testaments of the Twelve Patriarchs*), and Hebrew companion pieces to familiar "testaments" as well as the hymnody of Qumran (the hymns from Cave 1 and the apocryphal psalms, the many prayers and mystical texts). These compare readily to the plentiful literature in prayers and hymns that Judaism in general produced at this time.

The religious views of the people of Qumran, therefore, are not comprehensible in their particulars but rather in their fundamental orientation. Somehow these people understood their "faith" as the reflection and quintessence of these writings.

If this is so, then this cross section is all the more important for comparison with early Christianity. For then it is no longer a matter of the particular comparison of *the* "community" of Qumran with *the* Jesus movement, but rather it is a matter of the general expression of Judaism at this time in the religious testimonies of these texts. Thus, no special contact (or even identity) of particular Christians with the residents of Qumran can be presupposed; rather, the texts that are preserved here and the religious interest expressed in them are, in a certain sense, representative of the Judaism of that time in Palestine (and beyond). The question is no longer, How do the group in Qumran and the community of Jesus behave toward each other, but rather, How are the intertestamental literature and religiosity to be seen in relation to the religious views of the New Testament? That is our focus in what follows as we examine the Qumran texts.

Scholarship's limited focus on the "community" of Qumran came about because the only contemporary find was here. The mistake was in assuming that it applied only in this instance and only for this place, Qumran.

But the intertestamental texts are, for the most part, also found and transmitted outside Qumran. From them one could have long ago drawn conclusions about Palestinian Judaism at the time of Jesus. But the "conventicle" theses have displaced a stronger generalization. This was so the day before yesterday and yesterday, and it is still the case today.

As a result of all this, the study of the intertestamental literature in general would have to take on much more importance.

Part 2

Qumran and the New Testament

Chapter 4
Threat to the Faith?

In *The Dead Sea Scrolls Deception,* Baigent and Leigh give their material additional drama when they explain that it signifies a considerable threat to the Christian faith. "It had hitherto been believed," they write, that "Jesus' teachings were unique . . . 'good news' which had never been enunciated in the world before." They go on to ask, "Could he, casually and at a single stroke, undermine the faith to which millions clung for solace and comfort?" The authors picture the discoverers of the scrolls "handling the spiritual and religious equivalent of dynamite—something that might just conceivably demolish the entire edifice of Christian teaching and belief" (136, 137). Thus, the "Inquisition" has dated all textual discoveries in the pre-Christian era, "in a period of time" in which they somehow question or even undermine neither the New Testament nor the tradition. Repeatedly, Baigent and Leigh make mention of "opposition to the church's teaching."

Is not in fact the reluctant publication of the scrolls the best proof that something unpleasant was being withheld? Or is it simply a matter of an artfully constructed circular arrangement by the two authors: Because the texts are "dangerous for the faith," they had to be withheld from the public, and vice versa.

There is, of course, no text among the discoveries at Qumran (not even among the heretofore unpublished ones) that even mentions a single figure from early Christianity. But even if there were one, it would only express the perspective and point of view of its author. Nevertheless, what follows will attempt to explain why Christian biblical scholars and theologians do not tremble with every discovery of a manuscript but rather are even unable to find statements about the period of the Bible or "parallels" to biblical texts. For example, even if it were discovered on the basis of texts (which thus far has not been the case) that the "teacher of righteousness" had been crucified and had, according to the faith of his followers, been raised, that would not signify a precariousness to the position of Christians but rather an instructive analogy to the Christian faith; for faith in the possibility of the resurrection of martyrs, for example, belonged to the general belief of certain groups in the Judaism of that time.

In the Qumran texts there are, of course, abundant references that are extremely important for understanding early Christianity, and, in part, they have not yet been evaluated. Before we turn to them, the basic issue of a "threat to the faith" must be clarified.

Whoever artificially arouses anxiety over "parallels" is suggesting to unsuspecting Christians that they believe (or better: they *must* believe to please ecclesiastical authority) in something that is simply monstrously supernatural. Everything must prove to be absolutely divine in that it is completely new, wholly without analogy, without human emotions or limitations, of strictly timeless faultlessness, and completely independent of history. No doubt every intensive piety, and especially a fundamentalist piety, tends in this "Monophysite direction" (the so-called Monophysites denied the human nature and individuality of Jesus in favor of his divinity).

But it can be said without hesitation that in order to avoid precisely such a well-intended ever-higher place for Jesus, the church established the canon of New Testament writings. As a collection, all these texts frankly serve the purpose of forming a buttress against a detachment of the gospel from the concrete history of human beings. And since not only Jesus stood in this human history but also all biblical figures and "communities," their faith was always closely interlaced with the respective religious convictions of the nearest surroundings and its inhabitants. Thus, all piety has a necessary buttress in the surrounding matrix of the individual in his or her time and, therefore, Christian faith always exists in the tension between the two. If one does not keep this in mind, one isolates expressions of piety (such as the confession "Jesus is God's Son"), presents them to Christians, and says, "See, this is your faith." And then one attributes to such confessional statements precipitousness, transcendence, and absurdity. And hardly anyone knows anymore that at that time "God's Son" was a predicate for many figures (even in Judaism).

Conclusion: Whoever separates biblical declarations (and, in general, those of faith) from their historical connection or context makes them superhuman and inhuman, and in the end lets them become absurd.

"Revelation" need not always have to do with the completely new. Whoever said that God's Word always had to be something brand-new? Can it not also confirm and exalt what is old, trusted, and tested? Must God be appraised like a doctoral candidate who is expected to demonstrate new ideas? Would that not be too superficial an opinion? Would not one then, in fact, have to tremble with every new textual discovery? And indeed, would that not make what we mean by "God" absolutely distorted?

Can we not, rather, understand it as a confirmation of the gospel when love of neighbor and love of enemy are also the subject matter in other Jewish and Gentile texts from the biblical world? Must the Christian religion be profiled "against" the others or can it not much better assume its own shape in their midst?

By "assuming its own shape" I mean that which in early Christianity itself was seen as the attractive character in missionary work. This is not what was unique in religious-historical terms, but rather the manifest vividness of concrete human deeds and of suffering that was undeserved and patiently endured.

What is distinctively Christian and what is singular about Christianity is not new, unique ideas and programs, but rather the history of the influence of Jesus, the history of the relationship between Jesus and those who followed him. And what is unique is also not morally representative persons (the whole of the New

Testament quite clearly reports otherwise), but rather simply the uniqueness of this story itself. The history of the influence of Jesus is therefore unmistakable.

The uniqueness thus understood is, however, not an absolute that is removed from time. It is also to be distinguished from the significance that Jesus' message may have for me. The question then is whether and why something that is significant to me, something that strikes me as "truth," is not independent of whether and how this history of influence of Jesus reaches and affects me. Significance exists if I am able to live and die better with the example of life before me and the promise that accompanies it.

Our modern understanding of greatness and uniqueness is especially characterized by ideas of personal originality. Here our views differ demonstrably and quite clearly from those of the New Testament. For example, stories there of miracles (with slight variations) that the Old Testament told of the prophets are carefully retold— thus, the awakening of the dead in Mark 5:21–43 (Elijah and Elisha in 1 Kings 17:17–24 and 2 Kings 4:18–37), and the feeding of the multitudes in Mark 6:35–43 and 8:1–9 (Elisha in 2 Kings 4:42–44). The point is that the greater and more significant someone is, the more he or she resembles other great persons (of the past). The more similar one is to them, the more certain also is his or her legitimacy because it concerns the same handwriting of God. That is to say, precisely because one is a "copy" and of the same kind confirms his or her significance. The more intensively a great person realizes everything that one knows about others, the more his greatness is confirmed. Unlike the critical interpretation of the Bible since D. F. Strauss (*Life of Jesus,* 1835/36 and 1861), similarities with Old Testament accounts are no cause to declare a story "worthless." And the question of whether something actually took place cannot be decided in any case either positively or negatively. For people at the time of the New Testament the only important question was whether a bearer of all ancient promises was found. If he were simply there, the ancient stories and promise preceded him, so to speak; they formed the aura, the horizon, the only context within which he was to be understood.

And such would also be the case with contemporary analogies to the New Testament: To a certain extent, Jesus would have borrowed characteristics from every prophetic figure, every seer, wise man, and martyr that was known, because everything good and helpful that had legitimated those sent by God must and could now be incorporated by him. Wherever God is at work, clearly repetition is legitimate.

Moreover, that is an important distinction for our thinking. For us since the Renaissance and the Reformation, the domain of faith and religion must be as free as possible from "legitimate repetition"; instead, we find the latter (essentially since the same time period) in nature. Only personal creativity and originality still passes for faith and religiosity, and it is no wonder that the religious appreciation for the "poet" in the nineteenth and twentieth centuries is the final consequence of this religious esteem for the "original" and the corresponding devaluation of the law. It is entirely different in the New Testament.

Statements such as "There is nothing new" or "That can also be found elsewhere" or even "That was taken from somewhere else," therefore, do not in general concern early Christianity and its statements about Jesus in a harmful way. They are all to be roundly affirmed. But they do not explain what is crucial, namely, why it all was taken over, why one wanted and was able to apply it unconditionally to Jesus.

If a comparison may be permitted, it is as if a lovely woman is graced with the loveliest flowers and jewelry that can be found, only because all of this simply accentuates her beauty. For the "mysterious," the unexpected, and the fascination in a person can always be described only with old words that already exist. The shockingly surprising can only be defined with images that already exist.

And it says nothing against historicity, the actual occurrence of such events, if a similar occurrence involving other earlier prophets was told. Apart from that, the actuality, that is, the occurrence of events, was perceived differently by people at that time from the way we perceive it today, with the result that these questions cannot be decided at all on the same level of "experience."

Therefore, whoever would like to suggest to Christian theology that it must be afraid of discoveries of texts that bring parallels to light (and also, whoever then indeed also is afraid) has not understood what is crucial in the biblical message itself, namely, comprehending and fashioning religious reality in typologies, in ancient, traditional images.

If then the authors of *The Dead Sea Scrolls Deception* freely vouch for Father Roland de Vaux, that indeed his faith did not suffer because of the discovery of the texts, but that the scrolls themselves came to grief because of his faith, then the same thing, only surrounded by the suspicion of deceit, is suggested, namely, that someone found it necessary to falsify the texts themselves. But there is not a shred of evidence of that.

Moreover, "sexual suspicion" has also constantly played a significant role for the German public. Of course Jesus may have been married (to Mary Magdalene, naturally) and may have had children, and so on. Because there is not the least bit of proof of this, it is based on, among other things, the notion that all rabbis were required to marry. Regarding this matter, it must first be asked why this suspicion sparks such interest and is dealt with under the counter as a "big scoop." This suspicion has led directly to an interest in possible evidence that could be disclosed.

Centuries of Christian sexual education have led to the impression, still present in many places, that there is a competitive relationship between religion and sexuality which in religion is always decided to the detriment of sexuality. Therefore, extreme godliness excludes sexuality. How grateful we would be for any disclosure that would unmask this unpopular and oppressive rivalry at the root of Christianity as sanctimoniousness. All of the pent-up irritation could be relieved. Even the Protestant parsonage, present for generations, has not changed anything, in that such disclosures would be a blow against Reformation prudishness.

But, unfortunately, in the meantime there has been nothing to disclose. John the Baptist, Jesus, and Paul did not, as far as we can tell, fall under the commandment, only later imposed, that rabbis must marry, but rather they fell under the earlier traceable tradition regarding the virginity of prophetic figures, as it is reported in the Jewish tradition about the prophets Elijah, Ezra, and Daniel.

Chapter 5
Organization of the "Community"

We will now compare, passage by passage, statements from the Qumran texts with some New Testament texts. We will begin with the most concrete and then turn to notions of faith. It is important here not to stress the differences (naturally the people of Qumran did not believe in Jesus), but rather to see the early Christians as close relatives in the same family, as brothers and sisters among themselves and as cousins in relationship to the people of Qumran.

The Community as a Holy House

The designation of the community as a "body" is an image out of the scene of the then-current internal politics of the larger Roman Empire. That we do not find this image (heretofore) in the Qumran texts is surely attributable to the fact that the image is clearly of Gentile origin. But another image for early Christian communities, competing with and in contrast to the notion of the body, is preserved in Qumran: that of the house with walls, cornerstone, and foundation.

The so-called *Community Rule* describes the "community" thus: "It shall be that tried wall, that *precious corner-stone,* whose foundations shall neither rock nor sway in their place [Isa. 28:16]. It shall be a Most Holy Dwelling for Aaron" (1 QS 8:7–9; Vermes, 72–73). Like walls, cornerstone, and foundations, the community itself, seen as a whole, is characterized as something solid and therefore as a temple.

The same elements of a building are also mentioned in the letter to the Ephesians: "You are . . . built upon the foundation of the apostles and prophets, Christ Jesus himself being the cornerstone, in whom the whole structure is joined together and grows into a holy temple in the Lord; in whom you also are built into it for a dwelling place of God in the Spirit" (Eph. 2:19–22). Here also the concern is with the community, with the house, foundation, cornerstone, and temple. It differs from the Qumran text only in that foundation and cornerstone are interpreted allegorically, referring to apostles, prophets, and Jesus Christ. Thus, the letter to the Ephesians filled out the traditional image and differentiated it from a Christian perspective.

First Peter uses the same imagery to describe the church: "Come to him, to that living stone . . . ; and like living stones be yourselves built into a spiritual house, to be a holy priesthood. . . . The very stone which the builders rejected has become the head of the corner" (1 Peter 2:4–7). Again here the images of house, stone, cornerstone, and temple also refer to the church and to Jesus Christ. The points of contact with Ephesians are particularly close, inasmuch as mention was made there also of the entrance and the Spirit (Eph. 2:18), and both include the phrase "And you also" (Eph. 2:22; 1 Peter 2:5).

Like Jews, then, according to the Qumran text, early Christians understood themselves in terms of a temple, a holy house, when they came together. This does not mean that they rejected the Temple in Jerusalem but rather that they represented it. It was extremely important for these people that God had a house and that people gathered together were like foundations and walls that enclose God. It is a splendid view which unfortunately is lost to us today, but which we owe to the Qumran text and the two passages in the New Testament: that God keeps a space among the people, and that God then can live in their midst because together they are a sanctuary.

The Body of Twelve

According to the so-called *Community Rule* from Qumran (1QS), twelve men out of the whole of Israel played an important part in the group that is described here ("In the Council of the Community there shall be twelve men and three Priests, perfectly versed in all that is revealed of the Law" [1QS 8:1; Vermes, 72]). These twelve men were called the "House of Holiness for Israel," and the three priests the "Assembly of Supreme Holiness for Aaron" (1QS 8:1–6). Heretofore it was not clear whether the three priests were in addition to the twelve men or were included with them. From a newly accessible text, we learn that there were fifteen people altogether (4Q 251 3:7). The men were supposed to be distinguished by "perfect holiness"; to them fell the authority to teach because all special knowledge from the literature in scripture was supposed to have been imparted to them. They were thought of as the circle of founders; it is said of them that they were supposed to set themselves apart from the other, sacrilegious people, "and [they] shall go into the wilderness to prepare the way of Him" (1QS 8:13; Vermes, 72). They are characterized as a "precious corner-stone" and as a foundation. Their sheer existence atoned for the godlessness in Israel (1QS 8:10). Their relation to "Israel" is clearly discernible everywhere. The only question is whether this circle existed in reality or only on paper.

The twelve men with whom Jesus surrounded himself were also unquestionably representatives of the renewed Israel. According to Matthew, they are also portrayed as "perfect" (Matt. 19:21: "If you would be perfect" belongs with Matt. 19:28: "You ... will also sit on twelve thrones") and as having decision-making functions (Matt. 19:28: "judging the twelve tribes of Israel"). According to Luke, they are the leading authority for the interpretation of scripture because they were taught about scripture by the risen Lord (Luke 24:45: "Then he opened their minds to understand the scriptures"). Similar to the way the twelve in 1QS are called a "foundation," in Revelation 21:14 the names of the twelve apostles are inscribed on the foundation stones of the new Jerusalem. In the oldest testimonies, the twelve men whom Jesus assembled around him are not yet called "apostles."

Thus, in the first century B.C.E. and C.E. a renewal of Israel has been so conceived that it begins with twelve new representatives of Israel. They were something like counterparts to the ancient twelve patriarchs. (Jesus then would be in the role of Jacob.) They might be called "elders of Israel." In contrast to the body of witnesses for Jesus, the expansion by three priests depicts for 1QS perhaps a secondary form that developed later, since the contrast of Israel/Aaron is certainly not older or more original. But that Jesus entrusted the disposition of his message to the body of the Twelve at all is a remarkable and often too rarely considered fact. Jesus thus went back to the conceptions of his time for the shape, form, and, to some extent, also function of the circle of twelve.

Conclusion: The concept of the "concentric" renewal of Israel by means of a body of twelve men is found only in Jesus and a few texts from Qumran. Quite certainly there are close points of contact here.

The symbolism of the twelve tribes plays a special role in the *Temple Scroll* from Qumran. The organization of the administration of the Temple relies here fundamentally on the intact number twelve of the tribes of Israel. Thus the "heads of the clans of Israel" were to sacrifice twelve rams (col. 19), and from the homes of the tribes of Israel the first fruits of oil were to be offered (col. 22). In connection with a king of Israel, column 57 mentions a royal council, which was to consist of 36 persons: "The twelve princes of his people shall be with him, and twelve from among the priests, and from among the Levites twelve. They shall sit together with him to (proclaim) judgement and the law" (11QT 57; Vermes, 151).

Vis-à-vis the *Community Rule,* there were now represented also priests and (this is altogether new) Levites, each with the full number of twelve. The symbolism of twelve, stressed in the *Community Rule* and in the *Temple Scroll,* casts new light on the cultic character of the heavenly Jerusalem in Revelation 21–22 (God and Christ as temple) and on the role of the twelve names of the apostles for this city whose inhabitants will have a priestly character. But in view of the twelve disciples of Jesus and the three pillars of the primitive church ("temple"), namely, Peter, John, and James, one must also ask to what extent they represent the Temple or are appointed to serve in a new sanctuary.

In the same column of the *Temple Scroll,* mention is made of an assembly that was to take place on the day the king was enthroned. All men between 20 and 60 years old were to gather at an (army) camp led by "captains of hundreds and captains of fifties and captains of tens," and from them all the king shall select 12,000 warriors to be with him (11QT 57; Vermes, 151). To be sure, Jesus was also a "king," but he did not choose any warriors; he even rejected twelve legions of angels on whom he could have obviously relied (Matt. 26:53). And yet, in addition to the symbolism of twelve, the symbolism of the camp also plays a role in the Jesus tradition. We will now turn to the latter. In view of the symbolism of the twelve, it should also be noted that the text of the "multiplication of the bread," which is important here, ends with the statement that twelve baskets of food were left over (Mark 6:43).

The Camp

Mentioned only in Mark's account of the feeding, the observation that Jesus had the people sit down by hundreds and fifties (Mark 6:40) has so far been completely obscure. How was that practical? In reality we have here a typological way of thinking that was oriented to the salvation statements in the Old Testament. For in Exodus 18:21, 25, the camp of the Israelites in the wilderness was clearly organized in groups of 1,000, 100, 50, and 10. The New Testament writers take over the two middle divisions. But in the Qumran texts these same notions were also active at the same time. We have seen it in the *Temple Scroll,* and in 1QS 2:21–22 we read: "[A]nd thirdly, all the people one after another in their Thousands, Hundreds, Fifties, and Tens, that every Israelite may know his place in the Community of God" (Vermes,

63). Both in CD as well as in 1QM, it is repeatedly stressed that the people lived in a "camp" ("And if they live in camps according to the rule of the Land . . ." [CD 7:6; Vermes, 88]). The "camp" is their kind of "organization" because these groups saw themselves as representatives of the exodus into the new era of salvation.

Therefore, Jesus had the people who were also in the wilderness sit down in the arrangement of a camp. For Jesus also there was a correspondence to the exodus from Egypt; his feeding corresponds to that of the manna (see the interpretation of the feeding in John 6). The wilderness is the place of preparation for the new salvation.

According to the *Temple Scroll,* the camp will be established on the day when the king is enthroned. It is not surprising, therefore, that the motif of the camp and the desire of the people to make Jesus king (John 6:15), as well as the baskets that allude to the twelve disciples, appear together in the framework of accounts of the feeding. For the feeding of the multitude with bread was in New Testament times a sovereign, royal characteristic and privilege. That the twelve baskets refer symbolically to the twelve disciples has a parallel in the relationship of the seven baskets in Mark 8:8 of the feeding in a Gentile region to the circle of seven among the Jerusalem Hellenists.

Comparison with the Qumran texts shows precisely in the feeding accounts a striking accumulation of royal motifs, specifically in a cross section of the Gospels: the feeding itself, the division into camps (Mark), the symbolism of twelve, the key word "king" (John 6) in comparison to the note in the *Temple Scroll* that is concerned with the day of enthronement for the king. At the same time, however, in contrast to the texts from Qumran, the following becomes clear: For Jesus, any military aspect is remote; everything is purely miraculous. The characteristics of Jewish origin that are related to Qumran have been taken up and transformed in the image of a king as a "high-profile" miracle worker who has at his disposal a creative power of divine quality and, in addition, embodies in the purest way possible all the features of a gentle Hellenistic philosopher-king.

Conclusion: The revival of the notion of the camp calls forth recollections of the exodus from Egypt and, at the same time, contains a series of typically royal motifs from the immediate environment. Both reflect the expectation of an imminent era of salvation. Early Christians employed the same motifs and images as the writers of the Qumran texts, but the uniqueness of the kingship of Jesus becomes clear. Likewise the following aspect refers to the wilderness situation.

The Way of the Lord in the Wilderness

In Mark 1:2–3 we read the following about John the Baptist: "As it is written in Isaiah the prophet, ". . . the voice of one crying in the wilderness: Prepare ye the way of the Lord, make his paths straight." The Qumran text 1QS 8:13–14, quoted above, reads: " . . . and shall go into the wilderness to prepare the way of Him; as it is written, *Prepare in the wilderness the way of . . . , make straight in the desert a path for our God"* (Vermes, 73). In both cases Isaiah 40:3 is quoted, even with the same introductory formula, "as it is written."

As was the case with the exodus from Egypt, the wilderness is not the place of salvation, but it is the place of renewal and preparation for deliverance. For John as well as for the community mentioned in 1QS, the wilderness signifies separation from the lost masses of people; for both it is visible proof of the conversion that has been fulfilled. The word "conversion" is one of the most frequently employed words in 1QS, CD, the hymns, and the *War Scroll.*

Again, agreement is not merely external; it also touches on substance: the urgently necessary conversion for a radical new beginning. This conversion materialized in the period prior to Christianity through John the Baptist, who, not coincidentally, preached and taught in the wilderness.

Baptism and Immersion Baths

The relationship of the immersion baths mentioned in Qumran texts to Christian baptism is accepted as being much closer and more intensive than it once was thought to be. However, in this regard two traditions must be distinguished: baptism of repentance and baptism as a bestowal of the Spirit.

John the Baptist is justifiably seen as the founder of the non-recurring baptism of conversion by means of submersion in water. In comparison to other religious washings, this baptism has two distinguishing features: It takes place only once, and it is carried out by a "dispenser," thus by John as a prophet who is a "medium of salvation." Whether John as a priest (or a priest's son) actually lowered the candidate for baptism under water, like submerging a dirty dish into the water (as in Leviticus 11:32), seems doubtful to me. I think it far more likely that John sought the analogy to Elisha, the student of Elijah, for the Elijah-Elisha typology was familiar to the Baptist and to early writers about Jesus. John then baptized in the same way that the prophet Elisha did, according to 2 Kings 5:8–14, when he sent the leper to the Jordan to become clean by washing himself in the water seven times. Thus John himself does not submerge the penitent, but rather gives the command as a prophetic instruction. John might have combined this model of baptism in the Jordan in a special way with his preaching of repentance.

Some texts from Qumran (CD, 1QS, 4Q 414; differently: 1QM) also attribute a religious character to immersion baths. They were not one-time events and were carried out by the person who wanted to be clean. But, and this is decisive, in 1QS it is stressed again and again that (preparation for) repentance was the prerequisite to the immersion bath. Whoever submitted to the commandments of God was also allowed an immersion bath. This depicted, so to speak, the conclusion to the "removal" of an offense, indeed as a purification of the flesh. But the actual forgiveness of sins occurred beforehand by the "spirit of true counsel" of God (1QS 3:6–8; Vermes, 64).

In the newly available Qumran texts are fragments with prayers or hymns that were spoken at an immersion bath (4Q 414). In them is discourse about "atonement," "covenant," and the "holiness of God."

In common with the baptism of John the Qumran texts have the prerequisite of repentance; here as elsewhere we are dealing with immersion baths that are a tangible seal and representation of consummated repentance. The distinction lies obviously in the repeatability inasmuch as, according to 1QS, the washings did not at all occur in a context that was characterized by any particular notion of the end time. It was only the end-time orientation that postulated the one-time character of John's baptism and Christian baptism, and it is thus elsewhere in early Christian statements (compare the once-and-for-all character of Christ's sacrifice). One can therefore absolutely say that baptism by John was based on Jewish immersion baths as a sign of repentance, according to 1QS. It is similar with the death of Jesus in relation to other martyrdoms: In the end he appeases God's wrath. The decisively Christian element was a structural one: This washing and this martyr's death were the last and final ones, for God is so near that no infinitely extended linear time, in our sense, is any longer conceivable. And because they are binding commitments, they do not take place "privately" but rather through a representative of God. Baptism with John and in Christianity is no longer timeless and for that reason no longer takes place in one's closet but publicly; it is carried out in the presence of God's messenger of the last hour.

Qumran texts as well as the New Testament understood baptism with water as the completion of repentance. This relationship is stronger than the differences that have their basis in the different view of time of John the Baptist and Christians.

Baptism as the final reception of the Spirit is to be distinguished from John's baptism of repentance.

According to Qumran texts, the anticipated outpouring of God's Spirit will also be conclusive, as we read in the *Community Rule:*

"like purifying waters He will shed upon him the spirit of truth (to cleanse him) of all abomination and falsehood" (1QS 4:21f.; Vermes, 66). This outpouring will be a one-time event. It generally signifies the end of all evil, and it is not carried out by its recipients but rather by God as their counterpart. The Spirit of God is dispersed like water; thus it is an event similar to baptism. However, this event is not carried out here ritually but is to be understood, according to this text, as a graphic description of the end-time gift of the Spirit.

In contrast, the early Christians recognized an orderly baptism for the bestowal of the Spirit (for example, John 3:5: "born of water and the Spirit") that was to be distinguished from John's baptism.

When the two forms are compared, one can say that what Judaism, according to the text 1QS 4 quoted above, had formulated graphically as expectation was ritualized in the baptism of the early Christians (water baptism as a bestowal of the Spirit). One may therefore speak of the ritualization of a metaphor. Similar developments can also often be seen elsewhere in the early church and its sacramental rites. Thus, for example, out of the expectation of anointing by the Spirit in the rite of baptism comes an actual anointing, etc.

Conclusions: Baptism by John had many points of contact with the practice of immersion baths attested in Qumran texts, particularly with regard to conversion.

But clearly a relationship to later Christian baptism as a bestowal of the Spirit could also be seen. What is graphically formulated as an expectation of the end time in the Qumran texts was transplanted into the liturgy in early Christianity.

The two paths in which notions in the Qumran texts are restructured for a Christian doctrine of baptism are, therefore, the one-time-only character of rites and the ritualization of metaphors. The statements from the Qumran texts can therefore be seen throughout as older stages on the way to a Christian doctrine of baptism.

Ceremonial Feasts

In the countries to which we owe our culture, the common meal has been, since ancient times, the center of every community and the center of life. An expression of this is the Lord's Supper.

In the early Christian churches of the Pauline and the Lukan type, a common feast was plainly the most concentrated "reality" of the Christian life itself. Luke and Paul trace this community meal back to Jesus' instructions at his last meal ("Do this in remembrance of me"); Mark and Matthew also give an account of this meal.

Two texts from Qumran sketch a similar picture of the community. In 1QS 6:2–5 we read: "They shall eat in common and pray in common. . . . And when the table has been prepared for eating, and the new wine for drinking, the Priest shall be the first to stretch out his hand to bless the first-fruits of the bread and new wine" (Vermes, 69). Similarly, 1QSa 2:17–21 describes the meal for the end-time community that will have the Messiah in its midst: The priest shall say the blessing, and thereafter first the Messiah of Israel, and then all others according to their rank. This regulation applied to groups of ten or more men.

The similarities to the Christian meal are found in the following features: The common meal was an essential element of existence as a religious group. The director of the meal ("head of the family") said the blessing over bread and wine. Of Jesus, for example, we read: "He took bread, and blessed, and broke it. . . . And he took a cup, and when he had given thanks he gave it to them . . ." (Mark 14:22–23). And the text in 1QSa, intended for the end time, explains that the Messiah said the blessing at the meal. The person in the highest position—the head of the family or the host—always assumed responsibility for the blessing. Even at the meal with the Emmaus disciples, Jesus claimed the role of host and head of the family; he was recognized in this role by the disciples (Luke 24:30–32).

In every Jewish home the head of the family or the host says the blessing over the bread. In the Qumran texts as well as at the Last Supper and with the Emmaus disciples, this domestic custom is transferred to a religious circle that is not simply identical with the family.

The most significant distinction exists in that, according to the two quoted Qumran texts, the priest took precedence. But the precedence of the priest—also on other occasions—was a specific common characteristic in the Qumran texts, as we saw in the supplement of three priests to the circle of twelve. Early Christian texts corresponded to the more general Jewish expectation, since the Messiah appeared as the host and said the blessing.

The points of commonality can be explained in that under particular Jewish presuppositions (for example, when the head of the family says the blessing over bread and wine) early Christian churches as well as communities in 1QS and 1QSa perceived themselves above all as communities drawn together by a meal, not unlike ancient cultic societies (M. Klinghardt). For in such cultic societies it was customary to gather at regular intervals for common meals. These mealtimes were strictly ordered, especially with regard to leadership and finances. One can thus also say that the development of the Christian office cannot be imagined without the history of the community meal.

Conclusion: Contrary to our findings on baptism, there is no specific agreement between the Christian Lord's Supper and some of the Qumran texts that mention a feast. Rather, Christian community meals and the meals referred to in the Qumran texts were oriented toward common beginnings that were passed on by religious societies of this time. But wherever persons are organized into a society, boundaries to the society are always in the picture, thus giving rise to "excommunication."

Excommunication

According to Matthew's Gospel, Jesus already speaks of excommunication: If somebody who has sinned does not repent after personal counsel, then after a reprimand from two or three witnesses, and finally after public rebuke in the church, he is to be excluded, sent far away, and treated as a nonmember, "as a Gentile and a tax collector" (Matt. 18:15–17).

One can try to interpret such statements by Jesus as "inauthentic," but in doing so one then always presupposes something that cannot really be known, namely, the answer to the question of whether Jesus could have been thinking of something like his disciples living together in community at all. Or was he thinking instead only of modern religious individualists? In order not to oversimplify the answer, one should consider the fact that Jesus was a Jew, and first-century Jews thought of religion only as a community. Should Jesus have spoken of persons only in grand words and rose-colored tones and not also in terms of difficult relationships? Why must such things always be kept at a distance from him?

In one of his earliest letters, however, Paul already knew of a proper procedure for excommunication: Christians should come together and solemnly "deliver to Satan" the man who has sinned grievously, and for all to see (1 Cor. 5:5). Paul believed that Satan would physically destroy this person so that in this way his guilt would be expiated and he himself then be saved (for eternity). Only the burden of the transgression has to be destroyed by Satan and, to a certain extent, outside the church.

For both proceedings—that mentioned by Jesus and that mentioned by Paul—the closest known analogies are found in Qumran, among the newly discovered texts.

Jesus' statement in Matthew 18 recognizes stages of appeal: Reprimand before a second person, before two or three witnesses, before the church—then exclusion. In 1QS 5–6 and CD 9:3–4 almost the same procedure is found: Reprimand before a second person (with the emphasis not on punishment but on setting right), before witnesses, then presenting the matter before "many." Exclusion is absent in the texts from Qumran. In Jesus and the two Qumran texts, a definite, traditional interpretation of Leviticus 19:17–19 is offered: not to hate the brother and neighbor but to set him right; not to exercise revenge but to love. Obviously, it was necessary to describe more precisely the process of reprimand. And, according to Matthew, Jesus follows the same path as the two texts from Qumran.

What is the source of this commonality? For life together among Jews the text in Leviticus 19:17–19 was very important: Here we find also the command to love one's neighbor. At stake in "love your neighbor as yourself," which we can now better understand, is not at all some vague kind of love but rather the kind that takes into account the mistakes and lapses of the neighbor. And because that is a particularly delicate matter, the successive stages of appeal were developed, and developed in an interpretation of Leviticus 19:17–19 that serves as a common basis for use by Jesus and in the Qumran texts.

The place of the development of this commonality could have only been in Jewish communities that in this way wanted to shape quite seriously their communal life according to the law and the will of God.

That there is no mention of exclusion in the texts from Qumran indicates that one could not and did not want to exclude anyone: In contrast to Matthew, it was not a matter of missionary communities that were encircled by tax collectors and Gentiles, but of Jewish settlements with lifelong bonds.

The expression "church" (Greek *ekklesia*) in Matthew 18 could refer to organs of Jewish self-administration; the word is also used similarly in Sirach 23:24, where the issue is public censure before the "assembly."

That the assembled church, according to Paul (1 Corinthians 5), "delivers [someone] to Satan" has its closest corollaries in three Qumran texts of which two are new. The familiar one is 1QS 2:4–18 (Vermes, 63): There Levites curse "men of the lot of Satan" (i.e., men who henceforth belong to the fate and interest of the devil), who should be "cut off from the midst" (cf. also 1 Cor. 5:13, "Drive out the wicked person from among you") and "receive no forgiveness." The church answers this solemn curse with a two-fold Amen. As with Paul, it is a communal act of expulsion of evil persons and their consignment to the constituency of Satan.

In the newly available text 4Q 287 the devil (Belial) and his followers—that is, all children of the devil—as well as certain angels are condemned because of their "unclean impurity" (line 4), a particularly acute problem in Corinth, according to 1 Corinthians 5. Here also it is a solemn communal condemnation of the "opponent." A twofold Amen is the response of the community.

The most interesting text is now found in 4Q 266. It describes a proceeding, repeated every three months, in which a priest curses an evildoer in prayer. It says expressly: "Then he who was thus expelled must leave. And anyone who eats with him or even inquires about the condition of the man who was expelled should be revealed by the attendant in conformity with the customary practice, and his judgment will be carried out." In Paul it is almost identical: "I wrote to you not to associate with . . . , not even to eat with such a one" (1 Cor. 5:11).

There should also be mentioned here a list that contains similar notes just as they were quoted (4Q 477). Someone is named here who was rebuked because he "turned away from the spirit of the community" and "mixed" with persons or things that were not allowed. The two key words are also mentioned in 1 Corinthians 5: There are arguments for the suggestion that "spirit" in 1 Corinthians 5:5b refers not to the sinner but to the church. And the illegal mixing refers both to the offense for which he is excluded and to further association with him (5:11, "not to associate with").

Conclusion: We now know more precisely than before that for the church in Corinth Paul reaches back to a practice that we know only from the Qumran texts, but that must have been common in the Judaism of his time: a collective, communally exercised condemnation and expulsion of "children of the devil" who henceforth fall to his lot and are consigned therewith to death. The difference is only that, according to Paul, the new inner person of the condemned (here, his "spirit") is saved in the end. The condemnation is only one for his temporal existence but not one for eternity.

Having Only One Wife

Older scholarship assumed that the entire "community" of Qumran lived the celibate life of a monastery. Not many texts mention women. But we have already seen that these texts cannot be read into the reality of a "community." Today no one believes it was truly a celibate community. Among the new texts are finally some that mention parents.

At one point, however, there is a noteworthy and verbal agreement with Jesus' proclamation regarding the relationship between husband and wife: The familiar passage in Genesis 1:27, that God created human beings "male and female," is quoted in the *Damascus Rule* (CD 4:20–5:2) as well as by Jesus (Mark 10:6). It is interpreted as meaning that God created each man and each woman for each other, and this is taken to refer to marriage. Thus there is only one single legitimate union. But the agreement goes even further: Jesus prefaces his quotation of the Old Testament with the phrase: "But from the beginning of creation . . ." (Mark 10:6), and in CD 4:21 we read, "But the principle of creation is . . . " (Vermes, 86). Like the Qumran text, Jesus thus appeals to the (order of) creation and makes this the actual basis of his argument. Therefore, because the creation of human beings is in the singular (male and female), this is true for all time and for every marriage. It is precisely in this sense that God is also understood as the "best man" in the marriage of Adam and Eve. The relationship between Adam and Eve becomes the basic pattern of every marriage.

To this extent there is a commonality between Jesus' statement and the Qumran text. However, the application is different. The Qumran text forbids a man from having two wives within a lifetime. A man may be married only once, and after the death of his first wife he may not marry again; the same is true for the wife. It is different with Jesus. From the presentation of evidence, which he certainly took over from the oral tradition, he makes an argument against divorce. "What therefore God has joined together, let not man put asunder." He says nothing about remarriage after the death of a partner. The issue does not arise, and evidently Jesus permitted it. At this point he is less rigorous.

How can the very wide-ranging harmony between Jesus and the *Damascus Rule* here be explained? Did Jesus come from Qumran? Had he "gone to school" here? Hardly. Instead, it was likely that in the context of contemporary Judaism Jesus shared a stricter view of marriage with one of the texts from Qumran and based it also on Genesis 1:27. That means that the views of early Christianity, as a rule, were not derived directly and simply from the Old Testament as an interpretation, but rather they moved about in the context of contemporary Jewish interpretive practice. Jesus even participates in that here. He not only has the Old Testament (his "Bible") in sight, but he also interprets it as it was interpreted elsewhere in Judaism. What is "new" is only that he limits his interpretation to divorce, the prohibition of which is also included in CD 4.

Precisely here we see once again how important it is not only to look at the Qumran texts as products of an isolated "sect" but also to appreciate them as typical representations of more general currents of the Judaism of that day. Otherwise, neither the points of agreement with nor the deviation from Jesus' statements could be explained.

Chapter 6
Religious Practices

Saving Life on the Sabbath

Humanity was created on the sixth day, but the Sabbath is the seventh day of creation. With that it was clear that humans were not created for themselves alone and for work, but rather for the Sabbath and the joy of rest. The dispute in Judaism over the interpretation of the commandment regarding the Sabbath does not, therefore, concern details; rather, the meaning of human life revolves around the problems of the prohibition of work on the Sabbath.

In Luke 14:5 Jesus defends a healing on the Sabbath with the following analogy: "Which of you, having a son or an ox that has fallen into a well, will not immediately pull him out on a sabbath day?" The logic is the following: In spite of the prohibition of work on the Sabbath, one would save a child or a valuable head of livestock from a life-threatening situation. Even more so, then, Jesus should heal someone suffering from dropsy.

The Jewish discussion to which Jesus appeals is available to us through the Qumran texts. According to the *Damascus Rule* (CD 11:13–14, 16) regarding livestock we read: "And if [a beast] should fall into a cistern or pit, he shall not lift it out on the Sabbath." "A person who falls into a sinkhole or some other place no one should rescue with a ladder or any other means."[1] That

---

[1] *Translator's note:* Here I follow Berger's reading of this verse, which is different from that of Vermes. Whereas Berger's translation does not allow a person to be rescued on the Sabbath, Vermes's translation does: "But should any man fall into water or fire, let him be pulled out with the aid of a ladder or rope or (some such) utensil" (Vermes, 95).

means that freeing livestock is altogether forbidden, and human beings may not be rescued with the aid of a tool (but perhaps without a tool, e.g., with one's arms). What Jesus assumed in his argumentation as being allowed is essentially disputed in the *Damascus Rule*.

In one of the newly available Qumran texts, we find something different. According to 4Q 251 5–7 we read: "One may not rescue a head of livestock if it has fallen into water on the Sabbath. But if a person has fallen into water on the Sabbath, then he may throw him a piece of clothing to help him. But he may lift no tool on the Sabbath." Compared to CD 11 this text is "more liberal." By no means may persons be rescued by tools, but still pieces of clothing may be used, presumably from one's own disrobing.

For Jesus' declaration in Luke 14:5, the texts from Qumran can thus offer the following: They present the framework of discussion within which Jesus moves with his argument (forbidden work on the Sabbath; saving human beings or saving livestock; both for the case of falling into a ditch). The texts show that fundamentally there existed a latitude for decisions. It also becomes discernible that in the presupposition to his argumentation Jesus did not appeal to solutions found in the Qumran texts but to more liberal ones that could be based on Deuteronomy 22:4 (help for an ox or donkey; but there is no reference made to the Sabbath). As can be reconstructed from Luke 14:5, there was in any case in Judaism the view that persons and livestock could be rescued on the Sabbath from a fall into a ditch. This view would have been more liberal than that presented in the Qumran texts.

Later (fifth century C.E.), in the Babylonian Talmud in a passage regarding the saving of life on the Sabbath, we find the following: "If one sees that a child has fallen into a pit, one may sweep away the clods of earth and pull the child out; the faster, the more valuable the life, and one need not first seek permission from a court even if one builds steps to do so" (Babylonian Talmud, tractate *Yoma* 84b). Here is expressed what Jesus presupposed. The mention of steps (a ladder) indicates that the older discussion is not unfamiliar.

Conclusion: Jesus did not simply draw the commandment regarding the Sabbath out of the blue, but he knew (according to Luke) the discussion of his time and joined it. The Qumran texts, which also do not agree with each other, show that Jesus interpreted somewhat further the saving of human life than was allowed according to the contemporary texts that are known to us. Nevertheless Jesus did not claim for himself an unrestricted freedom.

The Poor in Spirit

The Aramaic-speaking community of Christians in Jerusalem is repeatedly described in the New Testament as being "poor." One spoke of the "poor among the saints in Jerusalem," and these persons were simply characterized as the "poor." When Paul gathered his collection, he said that it was for these "poor persons." It is disputed whether the church simply designated itself as "the poor ones" or whether as a whole it was truly "destitute." Bizarre theories have been derived from this, such as the notion that this church had been reduced to poverty because of communistic experiments. But that is not the point here. Above all, there is no indication that a community of Christians in Jerusalem called itself "the poor ones." The expression "the poor among the saints" in Romans 15:26 clearly assumes that not all were poor, but rather that there were poor persons among the Jerusalem Christians.

Persons in texts from Qumran are called "poor/humble." The Hebrew word *anaw* can mean both. This double meaning of the Hebrew word was significant in the first century c.e. because those who were pious and humble could hardly become wealthy since they did not cooperate with the Gentile occupation power.

So far, there does not exist a particularly close relationship with the early Christian church. One can only say that a religiously active Jew could not have become very wealthy. Early Christians and pious persons in the Qumran texts were in the same situation, and this situation is explained by the religious, social, and political climate. One speaks here of a "piety of the poor."

And yet, at one point there is a closer relationship. The first beatitude, in Matthew 5:3, reads: "Blessed are the poor in spirit, for theirs is the kingdom of heaven." In Luke this beatitude simply reads: "Blessed are you poor, for yours is the kingdom of God" (Luke 6:20). Many have puzzled over the meaning of "poor in spirit." A favorite popular interpretation understands it to refer to "stupid" persons while more exacting interpretations, suspicious of hypocrisy, see the verse as a reference to "internal poverty," that is, internal freedom from wealth, a poverty that is only spiritual and not actual destitution. In that case one would not even actually have to be poor but only to free oneself from possessions that, if one had sufficient possessions, posed no particular problem.

Now through the Qumran texts one can see how the first beatitude is to be understood. For in two texts from Cave 1 we find the expression "who are of a humble spirit." Thus in 1QM 14:7:

> He has taught war [to the hand] of the feeble
>   and steadied the trembling knee;
>   he has braced the back of the smitten.
> Among the poor in spirit [there is power]
>   over the hard of heart,
> and by the perfect of way
>   all the nations of wickedness have come to an end.
>   (Vermes, 119–20)

Here in one line we find those whose "knees are weak" (Vermes: "the trembling knee"), those who have a "bruised neck" (Vermes: "the feeble"), those who have "changed completely" (Vermes: "the smitten"), and even those "of a humble spirit" (Vermes: "the poor in spirit"). The relationship between righteousness and threatened and tormented existence is quite clear even here. What is crucial is that the "poor/humble in spirit" are not dull of mind or only internally poor, but what is at issue here is a religious character that is present in physical and psychic distress. This is also the case in Matthew 5, for the persecuted in 5:10–12 correspond to the "poor/humble in spirit." In the second passage, in 1QH 14:3, the "humble/poor in spirit" are parallel to "men of the truth" and "those who are purified"; in other respects this text presents many gaps. But in the same scroll of hymns mention is made of the "poor/humble of grace" (1QH 5:22), that is, of those who have received grace.

Conclusion: The "poor in spirit" in Matthew 5:3 are to be understood as oppressed righteous persons who are dependent, shattered, and in psychic distress. To be sure, the expression says nothing directly regarding the extent of material possessions, but indirectly it rules out the possibility of this being important. Only through the Qumran texts do we know anything about the content of these words. Like the expression "poor," the term "called" also refers to the religious and social self-understanding of the groups to which we now turn.

The Called

In the New Testament one often finds the church designated as "the called." But the Greek word *kletoi,* which we are careful to translate that way, has in the Greek a much narrower meaning, namely, "the invited," specifically in the sense of guests who are invited to a feast or banquet. But it has always been translated with the more general "the called" without any further explanation.

Only in the texts from Qumran does it become clear that "the called" are the same as "the chosen." Thus in 4Q 243, line 34: "In this time the called will be assembled." The context is an apocalypse of history regarding the end time (Pseudo-Daniel). Something similar was already known in CD 4:3–4: "The *sons of Zadok* are the elect of Israel, the men called by name who shall stand at the end of days" (Vermes, 85).

Conclusion: Only from the Qumran texts do we know that to be called is the same as to be appointed or to be chosen. The traditional translation intuitively hit upon the right meaning.

Until now, in another of Jesus' pronouncements one was able only to guess his meaning, namely, in a declaration that dealt with the question of exorcisms in early Christianity. There is almost no mention of exorcism in the Qumran texts. But the binding of the "strong man," an important image used by Jesus in this connection, becomes comprehensible only by means of the Qumran texts.

Binding the Strong Man

One of the most puzzling of Jesus' statements is the parable in Mark 3:27: "But no one can enter a strong man's house and plunder his goods, unless he first binds the strong man; then indeed he may plunder his house." The only thing that was clear was that this served as a foundation for Jesus' exorcisms. "Binding the strong man" had to mean confining the demon and thus rendering him impotent by means of powerful exorcising statements. Only then could persons be saved from what had possessed them.

In 4Q 532 there is the phrase "and the strong man shall be bound." The context has to do with the fallen guardian angels whom the demons brought to the earth. It was already known that they were bound. Enoch says to them: "It has been commanded to bind you on earth forever" (Ethiopic Enoch = *1 Enoch* 14:5; similarly in the Aramaic version of this book which was found in Qumran: "to bind you for all the days of eternity"; see also Jude 6).

Conclusion: In his parable of the plundering of the "strong man's" house, Jesus conforms to the jargon of exorcism. "Binding the strong man" means expelling the powerful (ringleader of the) evil spirit(s).

The Practice of Prayer

The decisive and most splendid religious and theological achievement of intertestamental Judaism becomes visible in its songs, hymns, and prayers, in its benedictions and doxologies. It is not at all understandable why early Christianity would have to be artificially separated from these testimonies of deep piety and lively faith in God. No, here is clearly expressed the "milieu" out

of which a messiah like Jesus and a passionate theologian like
Paul become comprehensible at all. To this succession of testimonies also belong the hymns from Qumran (from Cave 1; thus
1QH) and the exceedingly numerous prayers from Cave 4. Several examples will demonstrate this. From 1QH 10:5–12:

> Clay and dust that I am,
>> what can I devise unless Thou wish it,
>> and what contrive unless Thou desire it?
> What strength shall I have
>> unless Thou keep me upright,
> and how shall I understand
>> unless by (the spirit) which Thou hast shaped for me?
> What can I say unless Thou open my mouth
>> and how can I answer unless Thou enlighten me?
> Behold, Thou art Prince of gods
>> and King of majesties,
> Lord of all spirits,
>> and Ruler of all creatures;
> nothing is done without Thee,
>> and nothing is known without Thy will.
> Beside Thee there is nothing,
>> and nothing can compare with Thee in strength;
> in the presence of Thy glory there is nothing,
>> and Thy might is without price.
>
> Who among Thy great and marvelous creatures
>> can stand in the presence of Thy glory?
>> How then can he who returns to his dust?
> For Thy glory's sake alone hast Thou made all these things.
>> (Vermes, 192–93)

The person humbly confesses his condition before God. As in
Pauline theology the glory of God is the ultimate aim of God's
activity in general. From 1QH 11:22–32:

> Then will I play on the zither of deliverance
>> and the harp of joy
>> . . . and the pipe of praise
>> without end.

Who among all Thy creatures
  is able to recount [Thy wonders]?
May Thy Name be praised
  by the mouth of all men!
. . . .
There shall be neither groaning nor complaint
  and wickedness [shall be destroyed for ever];
Thy truth shall be revealed in eternal glory
  and everlasting peace.

Blessed art [Thou, O my Lord],
who hast given to [Thy servant]
  the knowledge of wisdom
that he may comprehend Thy wonders,
  and recount Thy . . .
  in Thy abundant grace!
. . . .
Rejoice the soul of Thy servant with Thy truth
  and cleanse me by Thy righteousness.
Even as I have hoped in Thy goodness,
  and waited for Thy grace,
so hast Thou freed me from my calamities
  in accordance with Thy forgiveness;
and in my distress Thou hast comforted me
  for I have leaned on Thy mercy.

(Vermes, 196–97)

This person gives thanks for the gifts of mercy and of the knowl-edge of God. He knows that praise and thanks in his relationship to God are, by themselves, acceptable.

The following text is one of the most beautiful of all from Qumran. It is a testimony to a "mystical" experience. The texts from Qumran—like those of the New Testament—intensively sup-port the phenomenon of early Jewish mysticism. Visionary texts of early Christianity such as the vision of the throne in Revelation 4 or hymns from the same book (for example, Rev. 7:12: "Blessing and glory and wisdom and thanksgiving and honor and power and might") become understandable with a broader background. From 4Q 286:

> The rest of Thy honor and the footstool of Thy majesty in the heights where Thou dost stand, and the rung of the ladder (at the beginning of the ascent to) Thy holiness; and the chariots of Thy splendor with their hosts and angels (which are) the wheels; and all Thy mysteries, foundations of fire, flames of Thy light, the brightness of Thy glory, burning fires of brilliant light and marvelous luminaries; honor and strength and majesty of Thy glory, the sacred mystery and place of the light; and the grandeur of the beauty of the source, majesty, and the center of power, honor, praise, and mighty acts and healings, and marvelous works, hidden wisdom and the origin of knowledge and the source of understanding, source of revelation and counsel of holiness, and hidden truth; storehouse of understanding for the sons of righteousness; and domicile of uprightness, those who fear God; and gathering-place of goodness and of those who fear God out of truth; and those who are forever merciful and the marvelous mysteries, when they appear. . . .
>
> (We bless) . . . the land and those who dwell (therein), . . . who inhabit it, the earth and all its parts and all its being . . . and all hills, valleys, and all streams, the magnificent land. We bless the depths of the forests and the wild deserts of Mount Horeb . . . and its wilderness and the foundations of the islands . . . , their fruits, the highland forests and the cedars of Lebanon, new wine and oil.

Of particular significance is the association in the first paragraph of the text of mystical vision with the experience of miracles and healings. It is precisely this that is also true for Jesus and for the apostles who were called (through visions).

The following section also deals with elements of visionary experiences.

On the Baptism and
Transfiguration of Jesus

In the newly available mystical texts regarding Levi (4Q 213, frag. 1, col. 2), we read in the provisionally reconstructed version (lines 18–21): "Their faces were shown to me . . . ; in the face of history I saw the heaven opened, and I saw the mountain below me, so high that it touched the heavens. And I was on it. Then the gates of heaven were opened to me, and the angel said to me . . ."

The concern here is experiences that resemble those of Jesus' baptism and transfiguration. At the baptism of Jesus it is mentioned that Jesus "saw the heavens opened" (Mark 1:10). At the transfiguration Jesus is on a high mountain (Mark 9:2) and near heaven. In the Gospel accounts as in the Qumran text this is the setting for heavenly pronouncements that are directed to the bearers of revelations.

Luke's version of the story of Jesus' baptism can also be made more comprehensible by the new Qumran texts. For in Luke 3:21 we read: "When Jesus also had been baptized and was praying, the heaven was opened." Only Luke mentions prayer. But a Qumran text (4Q 536, col. 1, line 6) also reads: "And a vision will come to him [i.e., Noah] while he is on his knees in prayer."

Conclusion: Qumran texts attest that Jesus experienced his central encounter with the realm of God in the framework of early Jewish mysticism. Once again this is confirmation that in the period of early Judaism regularity and conformity governed precisely in that area in which today we operate with the strongest and most intensive originality. That is also true for the expectation of the Messiah, which is discussed in the following section.

Chapter 7
The Messiah

Messiah and Son of God

Some of those who expressed their faith in texts of Qumran expected a Messiah. In that regard they were not alone in Judaism. There are also some interesting texts, though not very many, in which a messiah is mentioned. A number of these texts have only recently become accessible.

In one of the texts from Qumran, for the first time in Judaism we find mention of an end-time ruling figure who is called "Son of God." It is nevertheless possible that a messianic figure is meant. Until now illustrations of early Christian statements about Jesus have always been confined to Psalm 2:7 ("You are my son, today I have begotten you") and 2 Samuel 7:14 ("he shall be my son"), passages in which the title "Son of God" does not appear. An illustration of "Son of God" as a name for the Messiah would be new. (Angels and other figures such as, for example, Joseph the son of Jacob, could also be so named elsewhere.)

Because the text (4Q 246) has been and still is available only to specialists, it must be quoted here in my own translation. The brackets contain supplements to the fragments.

> 1 (1) . . . on him. He fell down before the throne. (2) [Daniel? said?:] King, why are you vexed, [why do you gnash] your teeth? (3) . . . your vision and everything forever. (4) . . . powerful. Oppression will be on the earth. (5) . . . Thus will be many massacres among the nations. (6) . . . the king of Assyria and the king of Egypt. (7) . . . he will be great on the earth. (8) . . . make, and

everyone will serve [him]. (9) . . . of the great one he will be named. By his name he will be called.

2 (1) He will be called the Son of God. And they will call him Son of the Most High. As the comets (2) which you saw, so will be their kingdom. They will reign for years on (3) the earth and they will suppress everyone and one nation the others. (4) Until the people of God rise up . . . by the sword. (5) His kingdom will be an everlasting kingdom, and all his ways will be in righteousness. He (it) will judge (6) the earth in righteousness, and everyone will make peace. The sword (will disappear) from the earth. (7) And every nation will bow before him. The great God is himself the power (8) and makes war for him. He will deliver all peoples in his hand. (9) He will throw them down before him. His dominion will be an everlasting dominion and all abysses . . .

The crucial statement here is in 2:1. Luke 1:31–32 reads very similarly: "and you shall call his name Jesus. He will be great, and will be called the Son of the Most High." The "be great" in Luke has a counterpart in the quoted Qumran text in 1:7, the mention of the name in 1:9. It could be that the person described in 1:7 through 2:1 is the "Messiah" to whom 2:5–9 would then also apply. In both cases the Messiah would be closely associated with his people.

But that is surely not the case. For the characteristics of this glorious kingdom are not exactly messianic: They will oppress everyone, and that will be nothing other than what the other peoples in the period of affliction before the end will also do to one another. And then if someone mentions the Son of God, it could also be a reference to a pagan attribution to a ruler (such as, for example, Alexander the Great). In that case, only the last part of the received text would refer to Israel (the period of peace at the end, beginning with 2:4), but then the "Son of God" no longer appears there.

Conclusion: If one takes as a basis the customary construction of apocalyptic texts, according to which the period of salvation and peace appears at the end, but is preceded by a time of oppression, the "Son of God" as Messiah appears here in the wrong period and therefore in the wrong place. Thus it is much more likely that in the Qumran text a pagan ruler is meant by its claim (perhaps Alexander the Great as ruler of Assyria and Egypt, countries mentioned immediately beforehand) rather than the Messiah of the Jews. Luke therefore (in 1:32) would have made use of a familiar style and the passage might be paraphrased in the following manner: "This well-known claim to be great and Son of the Most High is now fulfilled in Jesus. It is true for really no one else." Then the pagan claim of a ruler would be fulfilled in Jesus. If one explains the passage as referring to the Jewish Messiah, one then reaches the conclusion that Luke agrees with the Jewish expectations.

Age of the Messiah and the Raising of the Dead

One passage in the newly available Qumran texts contains a real sensation. Already here (and not first in the New Testament) is found in the series of deeds of the messianic period the hint that God (or perhaps even the Messiah) will make the dead alive.

We recall that in Matthew 11:2 mention is made of the "deeds of the Christ," and in Matthew 11:5 (as in Luke 7:22) these are then enumerated: The blind see, the lame walk, lepers are cleansed, the deaf hear, the dead are raised up, and the gospel is preached to the poor. This list of deeds originates from a combination of two texts from Isaiah: 35:5–6 (blind, deaf, lame, dumb) and 61:1 (poor, afflicted, brokenhearted, imprisoned). Isaiah makes no mention of raising the dead.

4Q 521 (frag. 1, col. 2) says of God (or even of the Messiah): (line 1) "Heaven and earth will obey his Messiah . . . (lines 8–12) he will release the captives, make the blind see, and lift up those who are cast down. Then he will heal the sick and make alive the dead and proclaim good news to the poor. He will guide the holy ones, he will lead them like a shepherd." Here we already encounter the raising of the dead, which the two Isaiah sources do not offer but which is contained in the lists in Matthew 11:5–6 and Luke 7:22.

This means that the Christian authors were not the first to expand the series originating in Isaiah. In the common source for Matthew and Luke, the so-called Q source, where the list perhaps first appeared, there was also no raising of the dead as an act of Jesus. Rather, it was a matter of expectations that had been associated with the messianic period a much longer time before. Therefore, the Qumran text represents a form of interpretation of Isaiah that is then found in Matthew and Luke. Moreover, in 11:2 Matthew describes this list as "deeds of the Christ," to which the expression "deeds of God" in line 11 of the document quoted here perhaps corresponds.

Conclusion: The expectation that in the messianic period the dead will be made alive was associated with the interpretation of the Isaiah passages in a Qumran text as well as in Matthew 11:5–6. Here we have a common (probably oral) tradition of interpretation.

While according to this Qumran text it was a matter of the deeds of God, according to other Qumran texts the charismatic dimension of the Messiah was at least expressed in that they spoke of the Messiah's gift of the Spirit.

Messiah and Spirit

Jesus was not a political-military messiah, but rather a prophetic one whose dignity was established "charismatically." In some texts from Qumran there are at least initial signs of such a view of a messiah.

In 4Q 287 3:13 we read: "The Holy Spirit descended on his Messiah." In the new text 4Q 521 (frag. 1, col. 2) the messianic period is also that of the Holy Spirit: (line 1) "Heaven and earth will obey my Messiah . . . and all that is in them. He will not turn away from the commandments of the Holy One . . . , (line 6) and his Spirit will hover over the *anawim* and the faithful will be strengthened by his power."

Because of the allusions to Isaiah 11:1–2 ("a shoot from the stump of Jesse"; "and the Spirit of the Lord shall rest upon him"), it is quite possible that 1QSb 5 depicts a blessing on the Messiah. For this passage in the Targum, the Aramaic translation of the Bible, is related to the Messiah. In 1QSb 5:25 we find: "you shall kill the godless with the Spirit of counsel and with eternal power, with the Spirit of knowledge and fear of God."

In the Qumran scroll 11QMelch we find Isaiah 52:7 quoted ("How beautiful upon the mountains are the feet of him who brings good tidings") and interpreted in terms of the "anointed of the Spirit": "And he who brings good tidings is the anointed of the Spirit . . . to comfort . . . and he shall instruct them." In addition to Melchizedek, considered earlier in political terms, a prophetically oriented end-time authority comes into view here (if the version of the fragmentary text is correct). One could very well also understand Jesus as the Messiah in the sense of such a "Messiah of the Spirit" and "proclaimer of the gospel."

The charismatic understanding of the Messiah is also made possible by the fact that in some longer-known texts and in a new Qumran text, prophets are characterized as anointed ones (of the Spirit): "And He made known His Holy Spirit to them by the hand of His anointed ones, and He proclaimed the truth (to them)" (CD 2:12f.; Vermes, 84); "the commandments of God given by the hand of Moses and of His holy anointed ones" (CD 5:21–6:1; Vermes, 87); new: 4Q 521, frag. 4, line 9: "and all his holy implements . . . and all their anointed ones."

Conclusion: In contrast to statements from the Old Testament, in Qumran there are clear references to the fact that "the" end-time Messiah or at least one of the messianic figures can derive his dignity by God's gift of the Spirit. These texts are of particular importance in answer to the question of how Jesus could be called the Messiah at all. As the Qumran texts attest, one was also able to call an essentially charismatically oriented bearer of authority "Messiah."

Various Expectations

In the Qumran texts there are a wide variety of expectations concerning the Messiah or messiahs. Some texts deal with a single figure, others with two or three end-time representatives of God.

According to the *Community Rule,* possibly three "messianic" figures were expected, for in 1QS 9:11, the order in the community was to be preserved "until there shall come the Prophet and the Messiahs of Aaron and Israel" (Vermes, 74). Besides a Messiah from Aaron (for the priests) and from Israel (for the lay people), in addition still another prophet was expected.

This finding is avowedly difficult to explain only for those specialists who assume a uniform dogmatic of "the sect." On the other hand, for first-century Judaism it was quite possible to expect two or three messianic figures (with separate responsibilities).

In view of this textual evidence, it is possible to ask whether the relationship between John the Baptist and Jesus might not be better understood in light of such expectations. For it is striking that Jesus and the evangelists assume no competition between the Baptist and the Messiah/Son of man, but rather allow both to stand with high position next to each other.

John the Baptist is portrayed as the son of a priest (son of Zechariah) and is thus of Aaronic extraction. And he almost has something of a parallel appearance with Jesus; in any case Luke consistently depicts him in that way.

Therefore, in the infancy stories in Luke's Gospel the "priestly" John is again and again sketched in parallel form to Jesus (for example, the surprising conception, visions, and angels). And yet Luke lets there be no doubt of the surpassing role of Jesus, who is portrayed emphatically in the same stories as a Davidic Messiah. Nevertheless, John is also later described by Jesus himself as the greatest "among those born of women" (Luke 7:28). It could thus be argued that by means of his consistent parallel portrayal Luke wanted to "uncover" at least the expectation that took into account a priestly and a Davidic Messiah.

In Qumran texts the Old Testament passage about the star of Jacob (Num. 24:17) is also associated with two different persons. The star of Jacob is explained as a reference to the "Interpreter of the Law," the scepter that shall rise out of Israel is identified with the "Prince of the whole congregation" (CD 7:18–21; Vermes, 89). There seems to be no connection here with the New Testament. The star seen by the Magi in Matthew 2 is not Jesus; it only points to him. 11QMelch, where Melchizedek appears with characteristics of a ruler beside the "proclaimer of the gospel," also takes into account two different end-time representatives of God.

Conclusion: The juxtaposition of Jesus and John the Baptist in Luke demonstrates that both early Christians and the authors of the Qumran texts reckon in the end with two important figures of authority, a Davidic one and a priestly one. However, among Christians the appraisal is the reverse of that in Qumran: In Luke the Davidic Messiah takes absolute precedence over the priestly one. But it becomes clear to what a great extent Christians themselves retain here the same expectations as are present in Qumran.

Similar expectations, but related to a single person, are evident when the issue is a Messiah out of Aaron *and* Israel.

The Anointed One
out of Aaron and Israel

Some of the texts from Qumran combine at least two of the figures mentioned above into one. They envision a Messiah (an anointed one) "out of Aaron and Israel." The coming Messiah was thus expected to be (in any case, also) of priestly extraction. This is consistent with the often-noted peculiar priestly "tendencies" of particular texts from Qumran. In some texts the priest assumes a higher place than the Messiah (if the latter is not a priest)—at the table blessing, for example.

The Christian tradition certainly acknowledges particular priestly characteristics of Jesus (such as his teaching in the Temple), but nowhere is his descent from Aaron asserted. Still, the following parallel is noteworthy.

In the letter to the Hebrews, Jesus is consistently described as a high priest, yet at the same time his descent from Judah is stressed (Heb. 7:14). According to the latter he would be, in the language of Qumran, a descendant of David and a Messiah for Israel. But according to Hebrews 7:11, Jesus' priesthood is legitimated, not by his descent from Aaron—as is stated in the same context—but "after the order of Melchizedek" (mentioned in Genesis 14 and Ps. 110:4). This means that, as in the Qumran texts, Hebrews considers it necessary to have Israel's Messiah also be a priest. For Jesus fulfilled his salvation and liberation in the priestly realm. Because a descent from Aaron cannot be demonstrated, Psalm 110, which was also commonly used elsewhere in early Christianity to describe the exaltation of Jesus, provided the reference to Jesus' majesty "after the order of Melchizedek," a priestly order, according to Hebrews, which rivaled that of Aaron. The result is that, as in some Qumran texts, the Davidic Messiah in Hebrews is also a priest. As is true there, his decisive work is as a priest. (But Jesus' priesthood is a different one, not the Aaronic-Levitical but that of Melchizedek; however, this figure is also not unknown in Qumran.)

Conclusion: Even early Christianity had no uniform conception of the Messiahship of Jesus. In particular, the letter to the Hebrews approaches the expectations of a priestly Messiah. Hebrews has a strong Jewish Christian character to it. But there is nothing to cause us to assume a special origin for the writer of Qumran. In contrast to Hebrews, in the Qumran documents the priestly expectations of a Messiah have nothing to do with the death of the Messiah. And yet there are new testimonies from Qumran regarding death by crucifixion.

Crucifixion according to the *Temple Scroll*

Only since 1977—after an adventurous prehistory—has the *Temple Scroll,* written on thin leather, been accessible. It contains an important new interpretation of the Old Testament regulation regarding "hanging on a post." In Deuteronomy 21:22 we find that someone is "hung on a tree" who "has committed a crime punishable by death." In the *Temple Scroll* this is made precise:

> If a man slanders his people and betrays his people to a foreign nation and does evil to his people, you shall hang him on a tree and he shall die. On the testimony of two witnesses and on the testimony of three witnesses he shall be put to death. . . . If a man is guilty of a capital crime and flees (abroad) to the nations, and curses his people, the children of Israel, you shall hang him also on a tree, and he shall die. (11QT 64; Vermes, 156)

The crimes here are betrayal of country (treason) and activity inimical to Israel among Gentiles. Now at the time of Jesus, jurisdiction for capital crimes rested in the hands of the Romans, so that in this area Jewish justice was meaningless. Nevertheless, the demand for Jesus' crucifixion could naturally have been based on Jewish presuppositions of this kind, as described in the *Temple Scroll*. For example, Jesus' words about the destruction of the Temple (Mark 13:2; 14:58) could have been understood as a prophetic curse directed against Israel. That would clearly be a "curse of the people" in the sense of the *Temple Scroll,* quite similar to the prophecy "against this city and against this land" on account of which the prophet Uriah (according to Jeremiah 26:20–24) was to be condemned. Such an act could only encourage the Romans. In any case, the basis for the delivery of Jesus for crucifixion was a political one to settle tensions between Jews and Romans. To that extent the passage from the *Temple Scroll* is significant.

In one passage from the newly available Qumran texts, it is not clear whether the Messiah from the house of David kills or is killed. 4Q 285, frag. 7:4, reads: "And they will kill [or, it will kill] the leader of the community, the shoot of David [or, the leader of the community, the shoot of David, will kill them]." As always, the Messiah here is involved in bloody, end-time confusion. In any case, the Messiah of Israel is always a descendant of David, according to the Qumran texts.

The Shoot of David

Several Qumran texts contain important indications that suggest an active expectation of the arrival of a Davidic Messiah in the intertestamental period. Such an expectation was by no means obvious because, as is well known, there were also expectations of the end without a Messiah.

In the above-mentioned text (4Q 285, frag. 7), Isaiah 11:2 ("And the Spirit of the LORD shall rest upon him") is quoted and is applied to the Messiah, the shoot of David, and then the discussion turns to judgment.

In 4Q 252 the "Messiah of righteousness, the shoot of David" comes, for whose sake covenant and kingdom have been given to Israel whenever, and because, Israel has kept the law.

Apart from special messianic expectations, one finds in the new Qumran texts examples that support the old assumption that the image of Jesus in the Gospels is plainly drawn essentially according to that of the "righteous one."

New Allusions to
the Johannine Christ

In 4Q 416 1:4–5 what is said about the righteous one is true of Jesus in John's Gospel: "Thus he [God] glorified it as you were consecrated for him, as he made you a Holy of Holies . . . he decreed your fate and greatly increased your glory and made you his first-born among . . . " Previously it was said: "He separated you from all bodily spirits," "he separated you from human beings," and "he gave you authority." Associations are particularly found with John 17: The Father glorifies the Son (v. 1) and gives him authority (v. 2). The Son is consecrated to the Father (v. 19). Jesus is called firstborn (John 1:18), and he applies to himself attributes of the Temple (John 7:37).

Conclusion: Many heretofore quite mysterious elements of John's Gospel become more comprehensible when they are understood as statements about the specially elected righteous one in the sense of this Qumran text.

According to Paul, Christ stands as the righteous one vis-à-vis Adam, through whom sin entered the world.

Adam and Christ

Whenever Paul wants to emphasize the universal significance of Jesus, he contrasts Adam and Jesus Christ (see Romans 5 and 1 Corinthians 15). Both figures correspond to each other. Jesus corrects what Adam brought about; he surpasses Adam in a positive way; and actually Jesus is the perfected Adam, the first human being as he was truly intended to be. The Qumran texts certainly do not know this kind of typological juxtaposition between Adam and the Messiah, but they do indeed provide a very important and thoughtful groundwork for the Pauline comparison. Again and again the issue is that God will transfer "all of Adam's glory" to those who are redeemed at the end and are purified by the Holy Spirit, or that God takes away the sins of human beings and lets them inherit "all the glory of Adam" (1QS 4:20–23; 1QH 17:15; CD 3:20).

To be sure, in these texts there is no single figure of a second, final Adam. But it will still be the "glory of Adam" as a collective gift that is given to all the redeemed. Even Paul can talk about glory, or splendor, in connection with the new, second Adam (1 Cor. 15:43: "raised in glory").

Conclusion: Beginning and end correspond to each other. At the end we come around to Adam again. Everyone will then receive what was lacking or lost in the first Adam. What in some Qumran texts will be a collective gift to everyone is understood in Paul finally also collectively, but is tied to the irrevocable mediation by means of the one mediator, Jesus Christ as the second Adam.

Chapter 8
Sons of Darkness and Children of Light

Humanity before God
according to the Qumran Texts

A Bit of the Christmas Story

The last words in "Glory to God in the highest," sung by the angels, according to Luke 2:14, were for a long time a puzzle over which the churches were greatly divided. After "Glory to God in the highest" did the angels intend to say: ". . . and on earth peace to people of goodwill" (as in the Latin of the Vulgate)? Or did they intend to say, ". . . and peace on earth, goodwill to humanity"? (According to Martin Luther and his commentary, goodwill to humanity is "the divine goodwill or the goodwill . . . that through Christ God has toward humans"; but it is also "the peaceful heart that finds pleasure in all things.") Or, finally, did the angels intend to say, ". . . and peace on earth to persons of the divine goodwill" (those in whom God is pleased because God "desires" them and chooses them)?

The passage was controversial confessionally because some (Catholics) saw the goodwill of humanity compensated, and others (Reformed) found confirmed God's sovereign right of election independent of human merit. The fundamental question was, therefore, about what was at stake: God's will vis-à-vis human beings, or the good, grateful will of human beings. Apart from the fact that the confessions are not disputed so much today, the Qumran texts have for the first time provided the possibility of deciding this question and of doing so in the sense of the electing will of God.

In the texts from Qumran there is the phrase "sons of his good will/estimation," as in the hymns: "the abundance of His mercies / towards all the sons of His grace" (1QH 4:32–33; Vermes, 177; and quite similarly in 11:9). In 1QS 8:6 the "elect of Goodwill" are mentioned (Vermes, 71). That means that God has elected persons according to his free decision. One can now conduct oneself according to God's estimation or to God's goodwill, but in all cases God's will is the standard.

Conclusion: The song of the angels in Luke 2:14 reads: "Glory to God in the highest, and on earth peace among persons whom God has chosen according to God's goodwill." Such persons are those to whom God wishes to grant salvation, certainly all those whom the gospel reaches. Similarly, according to the texts from Qumran, God grants mercy to human beings.

But election presupposes that there are also those who are not elected. And some Qumran texts are characterized by a "dualism," a division of persons into those who belong to God and those who belong to God's opposite.

Children of Light

Only a few writings from Qumran offer a distinct dualism as a view of the fundamental division of reality into two parts: 1QS and 1QM, as well as 4QTAmram (*Testament of Amram*) and 4Q 462. The restriction of dualistic statements to so few texts demonstrates once again that the books of the residents of Qumran are not theologically uniform.

In 1QS and 1QM there are children of light and children of darkness, to which correspond spirits of light and spirits of darkness, spirits of truth and spirits of wickedness. At their head are the prince of light and the angel of darkness, respectively. Human beings then walk either paths of light or paths of darkness. They carry out corresponding works, and we find, juxtaposed to each other, lists of such works (for example, humility and patience vis-à-vis greed and laziness), so-called catalogs of virtues and vices.

The children of light are supposed to "hate" the children of darkness, that is, they are to separate and distance themselves from them. An end-time struggle of destruction will be carried out against the children of darkness. "Until now the spirits of truth and falsehood struggle in the hearts of men" (1QS 4:23; Vermes, 66).

Consequently, in the texts we find a cosmological dualism based on the spiritual world, as well as an ethical dualism based on human works. Earlier one spoke of a "dualism of decision," but that is scarcely employed anymore because the texts are aimed at persons who have already decided; on the other hand, this dualism is also not static. Rather, these dualistic statements make the elite "elected" minority alert to their danger, enjoin their spirit of resistance, and exhort them to a conduct that corresponds to their status. For the struggle and the threatening temptation to fall away do not come to an end but are still present. In view of this trajectory of the text, it is also apparent why a "conversion" of the children of darkness is not under discussion. Such a consideration lies beyond the intention of the texts, even when the matter hardly seems unrelated.

Conclusion: A dualism as in these Qumran texts, a division into sons of darkness and children of light, is found when the group of the children of light find themselves in a minority situation, threatened from without and within (through the conflict in one's heart), and a victory is by no means already won. They actually need separation from the others and are therefore summoned to hatred.

The closest analogies to many early Christian statements are present here. Above all, this is true for Paul and the Gospel of John. In his speeches of exhortation, Paul reminded the churches that they are children of light and do not belong to the darkness (1 Thess. 5:4–11). He admonished the Romans to put away works of darkness and to put on the armor of light (Rom. 13:12), and he suggested to his opponents in Corinth that Satan had disguised himself among them as an "angel of light" (2 Cor. 11:14). In 2 Corinthians 6:14–15, he asks what righteousness has in common with lawlessness, light with darkness, Christ with Belial. With "Belial" he uses a name for the hostile spiritual power that we also know from the Qumran texts.

In these parallels, therefore, Paul is either engaging in polemic against his opponents or (for the most part) in basic exhortation. Ephesians 5:8 can also be understood in a very similar way: "for once you were darkness, but now you are light in the Lord; walk as children of light." There follows again a list of the fruits of light.

In John's Gospel the dramatic struggle between the darkness and light, in which persons, as in the Qumran texts, participate by their works, is mentioned repeatedly. The darkness has not "overcome" the light (John 1:5). Judging by their works, people love darkness more than light (John 3:19–21). Jesus exhorts those with him to walk in the light "that you may become sons of light" (John 12:35–36).

In Luke 16:8 Jesus contrasts the "sons of light" with the "sons of this world." In the context Jesus dualistically sets service to mammon against service to God.

Conclusion: At times the discussion of light and darkness has to do with the self-estimation of a small group that is threatened internally and externally. Paul and John come especially close to some of the Qumran texts. A sure indication is always the presence of the self-designation as "children of light."

How are these important similarities to be explained? At this point people used to engage in risky and unprovable speculations about connections of "the" community of Qumran to (the communities of) John and Paul. However, on the basis of our considerations, the compulsion to give geographic definition to these writings, or even to the trains of thought assimilated in them, falls away.

A simpler explanation could be that light is a "concept of enlightenment" that is bound to an acquired understanding. Thus again and again conversion (to the true God) is understood as a transition from darkness into light. In the texts mentioned above, it can be easily shown that at issue are persons who not too long before had changed their religious status, having come from darkness into light (or who were challenged to do so, as in

John 12:35–36). Thus, before he speaks of the works of darkness and the armor of light, Paul mentions the moment "when we first believed" (Rom. 13:11). Such persons are still endangered in their newly won status and therefore must be reminded where they belong. Whenever conversion is discussed within the Judaism of that time (be it among proselytes or in reference to intra-Jewish reform movements to which I assign 1QS and 1QM), references to light and darkness and the children of light consequently belong to a kind of specialized terminology. Thus, one also speaks of Abraham and Job, who are converted to the God of Israel and to Judaism (and thus become "proselytes"), with the result that after deep darkness they have now seen the light. In his conversion Paul also sees Jesus as light.

Through the use of this dualistic language, early Christians such as Paul and John indicate that they understood Christianity as a movement of reform and conversion within Judaism that was internally aimed at conversion (thus as John's Gospel) or outwardly directed as in Jewish proselytism (thus Paul).

By no means did one have to have been for a time a member of a fictitious monastic community from Qumran in order to talk about "children of light." It was enough to be concerned with "conversion." But to describe something like this, a certain language was needed that in this case was not available in the Old Testament because there was no such thing. This metaphorical, graphic language was developed in certain circles of Judaism at the time and taken up by early Christians because early Christianity was first and foremost a radical religion of conversion.

Agreement with regard to the notion of the new covenant points in a very similar direction.

New Covenant

The group that is evident in the *Damascus Rule* called itself "New Covenant." This is the only Qumran text in which this expression appears, and it appears regularly in the form "entering the new covenant in the land of Damascus." 1QS also has to do with entering the covenant, but there is no mention there of the "new" covenant or of Damascus.

The term "new covenant" in CD could, but does not necessarily, go back to Jeremiah 31:31–34 where the new covenant is promised; in any case the passage itself is not quoted. But in Jeremiah 31:33–34, this covenant is distinguished by the fact that God's commandments are followed and kept. The same is the case in the program of the *Damascus Rule:* "For all who walk in these (precepts) in perfect holiness, according to all the teaching of God, the Covenant of God shall be an assurance . . ." (CD 7; Vermes, 88).

Even early Christian churches took on the language of the new covenant for themselves (Paul, Luke, Hebrews). In this respect Jesus' death is of foremost importance, but Paul also talks about the new covenant of the Spirit (2 Cor. 3:6). The words at the Last Supper in Mark and Matthew are only concerned with the covenant of Jesus ("my covenant"). A reference in Hebrews 8:8–12 to the forgiveness of sins quite clearly is based on Jeremiah 31:34.

In each case the new covenant signifies the decisive end-time turning point and the fundamental renewal of the relationship to God. There is in the New Testament in Paul at least an implicit association with the keeping of God's commandment when in 2 Corinthians 3 the covenant of the Spirit, as shown in the formula "not the letter but the Spirit," includes a new relationship to a kind of preservation of God's commandment. And as for the Gospels, it could still be the case that the transfiguration scene, which is patterned after the Sinai event (mountain, cloud, appearance of Moses), with God's instruction "Listen to him," is a new form of the covenant relationship in that one now finds God's will in Jesus' word. And in light of this scene, Jesus' violent death could then (simply) be the sign of the covenant (as the blood in Ex. 24:8 is for the Old Testament). The New Testament emphasizes, however, in each case the bloody act of the realization of the covenant, which is newly sealed in the death of Jesus. And even if the (covenantal) law is not abolished, the manner of its fulfillment is more strongly characterized as something new in the New Testament than in the *Damascus Rule*.

Conclusion: What early Christian texts have in common with the *Damascus Rule* is that generally the important dimension of the new covenant is put forward. Thus, both groups see themselves as bearers of the end-time renewal, and in each case this also includes a perfect preservation of God's will. But early Christianity then stresses very strongly the bond to Jesus' word (which has to do with God's will), Jesus' death (which has to do with the formal conclusion of the covenant and the forgiveness of sins), and the Spirit from Jesus' resurrection (as the strength to fulfill the Torah). To this extent the new Christian interpretation of the common good is quite distinct at this point.

Holy Spirit

The Spirit of God is incomparably more significant for the New Testament than for the Old Testament. A tendency toward this important change is evident in Judaism, precisely in the Qumran texts. Above all, the Qumran texts belong to the very few examples in Judaism in which an end-time outpouring of the Spirit is expected (1QS 4:21). There is also now an example in 4Q 521 (frag. 1, col. 2, line 6): After the Messiah is mentioned, we read: "And his Spirit will move over the poor/humble, and he shall restore the faith by his strength." This passage is extremely interesting because the movement of the Spirit "over" the humble corresponds to the movement of the Spirit of God over the waters in Genesis 1:2. At issue, therefore, is a "new creation." Just as in Paul, the Spirit of God causes it. And also, as in Paul, the Spirit provides the power.

The Holy Spirit of God brings joy to humanity (1QH 9:32). Joy is one of the central gifts of the Spirit in Paul. Again and again it is the Holy Spirit that purifies human beings (1QH 4:21, here parallel to "grace"). Thus particularly also as the final purification (1QS 4:21) it is "sprinkled" (like a liquid) over God's servants

(1QH 17:26; 1QS 4:21). In early Christianity God's Spirit always purifies when it is bestowed in baptism. That is formulated with particular emphasis in the statement of John the Baptist, according to which one is to come who will baptize with the Holy Spirit (Mark 1:8).

Those "anointed of the Spirit," namely, the prophets, and the "anointed one of the Spirit," an end-time prophetic messianic figure, were already familiar. What is new is that the Holy Spirit of God now rests on the Messiah (4Q 287).

The admonition in Ephesians 4:30 not to "grieve the Holy Spirit" corresponds to the admonition in Qumran: "Do not decrease your Holy Spirit in your affairs (and) do not exchange your Holy Spirit for any riches, for there is no price for your life (your soul)" (4Q 416 9:2/10:1, 6). At the same time, the passage has similarities to Mark 8:37, according to which people can give nothing in exchange for their soul (life). Here also belongs CD 7:3f., according to which one is not to defile one's holy spirit. The *Shepherd of Hermas*, a document written in Rome about 120 c.e., admonishes people again and again not to trouble the Holy Spirit within themselves.

Conclusion: In the Qumran texts, the Holy Spirit plays a large role. This similarity with the New Testament is based on the fact that the writers believed that God's Spirit would be granted particularly with conversion. Conversion is a renewal of life by means of the divine Spirit.

Because early Christianity as well as many witnesses from Qumran fostered a conversion, not only did the Holy Spirit play a comparatively large role but also much is said about sin and righteousness.

Sin and Justification

Important insights into the human situation before God are offered in a relatively large number of texts from Qumran that could be characterized as building blocks for the Pauline doctrine of justification (comprehensively understood). These commonalities—as well as the new Christian peculiarities of Paul—should not be obscured by the basic assumption that the Qumran texts are somehow necessarily "legal" and Paul is somehow "against the law." Rather, the Pauline position toward the law cannot be defined so simply, and, seen as a whole, it proceeds along the edge of what has been discussed here. That is also important for Paul's interpretation itself.

Fundamentally, the distinction between God and humanity can be thus defined:

> For thine, O God of knowledge,
>   are all righteous deeds
>   and the counsel of truth;
> but to the sons of men is the work of iniquity
>   and deeds of deceit.
>   (1QH 1:26–27; Vermes, 167–68)

That humans are sinners and God is righteous is also Paul's point of departure (see Rom. 3:9). Again: "And what is a man of Naught and Vanity that he should understand Thy . . . deeds?" (1QH 7:32; Vermes, 186).

Therefore, here as there, the only hope resides in God's mercy:

> For I know there is hope in Thy grace
>   and expectation in Thy great power.
> For no man can be just in Thy judgement
>   or [righteous in] Thy trial.
>   (1QH 9:14–15; Vermes, 190)

Alongside this one might read Romans 3:20–24, with its central assertion that no flesh is righteous before God and something can be made righteous only by God's grace.

> and I know [that] righteousness is Thine,
>   that in Thy mercies there is [hope for me],
>   but without Thy grace, [destruction] without end.
>   (1QH 11:17–18; cf. 7:16–18; Vermes, 196)

As with Paul, in its distance from God, humanity is viewed extremely realistically as flesh, and this stands in direct relationship to sin and death: "Thy marvelous mysteries . . . what is flesh (to be worthy) of this? . . . he is in iniquity from the womb. . . . I said in my sinfulness, 'I am forsaken by Thy covenant' " (1QH 4:27–30, 35; Vermes, 176–77).

The relationship between flesh and sin becomes most evident with Paul in Romans 7:14 where he says, "but I am carnal, sold under sin." In 4Q 416 3:7 the "drive of the flesh" is now also illustrated, a prelude to the "evil impulse" of the rabbis.

Thus there is even the "spirit of flesh" (1QH 13:13; 17:25; and also in 4Q 416 1:1), which stands opposite the Holy Spirit (1QH 17:26). Holy Spirit and flesh are defining contrasts in Pauline theology.

Conclusion: The human situation before God is defined by flesh, sin, and absence of righteousness, an existence of dust. In contrast, God shows humans grace, mercy, and glory and grants them the Holy Spirit. God is the righteous one opposite them. Mediating between the two is humanity's hope, expressed in prayer.

In the midst of this basic constellation Paul constructed his theology. Paul's most important contribution was that he located God's grace and mercy in the person of Jesus Christ, in his death for our sakes.

The newly available Qumran texts, moreover, contribute very significant strands of thought which, without proof or example, were heretofore simply attributed to the Judaism out of which Paul came.

So now for the first time the expression "works of the law" is found in a pre-Christian Jewish source. Paul uses this expression, for example, in Romans 3:28 where he writes that "a man is justified by faith apart from works of law," (similarly in 3:20). In Qumran we read: "And finally we wrote earlier for you regarding particular works of the law which we considered for your own good and for that of your people, for we see that you possess the gift of discernment and knowledge of the Torah" (4Q 397, lines 29–31). According to this text, "works of the law" are special, not generally familiar paths to fulfillment of the Torah that were inferred from the Torah. From the New Testament, an example would be the prohibition of divorce in Mark 10:2–12 which, as we have seen, was derived from the Torah (namely from the creation story). Also, some of the antitheses in the Sermon on the Mount would be "works of the law" in this sense.

The closest known pertinent analogy to Paul's mention of the works of the law in relative temporal proximity were, up to now, the "works of the commandments" in the Syriac Apocalypse of Baruch 57:2 (=2 Baruch; end of the first century c.e.). The discovery in Qumran confirms that Paul refers here to a current Jewish way of speaking. A work of the law in the sense used here is, therefore, a concrete deed of fulfilling the Torah, a specific way of following the Torah.

Also in 4Q 397 the author writes that the deed will be imputed as righteousness (lines 33–34): "Then you will rejoice at the end, when you will find that particular words of ours were true. It will thus be imputed to you as righteousness that you did what was right and good before him, for your own good and for the good of Israel." This text is also important because here the act is "imputed as righteousness." In Genesis 15:6, in contrast, regarding Abraham we read that his faith was imputed to him as righteousness.

Now this passage from the Qumran text is not a "repudiation" of Genesis 15:6 but rather only a contemporary interpretation. For there was no difference between faith and action; both were an organic unity. The letter of James directly illustrates the same interpretation of Genesis 15:6. According to James 2:21, it is the case that Abraham was "justified by works" because faith took form in works. For contemporary Judaism there was no contradiction here.

In any event one may ask whether Paul introduced a contradiction here. But first it should be said that for those who were Christians faith and works clearly belonged together, even according to Paul. Faith is set into action by love (Gal. 5:6). Faith without works, according to Paul, would be impossible.

Only if one is not yet a Christian does Paul say: Not by works under the law without, before, or beside Christ, but rather by faith in Christ alone does anyone attain the status of a justified person, of a person accepted by God. To this extent is faith alone "imputed" for the fundamental question of nearness to God.

In the newly accessible text 4Q 458, we read of a group of persons at the end time who "were justified and lived according to the laws" (frag. 2, col. 2:4). It is not clear by what means this justification was effected. Living according to the laws is perhaps seen as a consequence made possible thereby. That is also the case for justified Christians. Perhaps the two stand side-by-side and are simultaneously true.

Conclusion: All the problems as well as the vocabulary of the Pauline doctrine of justification in particular were in circulation in the Judaism of the time. What is new in Paul is that the anticipated grace in the Christ event has already been "made secure." And Paul defines the basic access to God as "faith alone." Whoever sees a different access sets it in strict opposition to the path of faith. And only in this regard can there be an opposition between faith, on the one hand, and works or works of the law, on the other—that is, only if one wants to introduce or play off the latter against faith and its absolute, irrevocable priority. But in other respects this faith is expressed in works and is thus—by the power of God's Spirit—a fulfillment of the law. Paul stands in opposition to Qumran, therefore, when he insists on the pointed priority of faith, which naturally can only be faith in the God who raises the dead. That Paul chose this path has less to do with his mission to the Gentile nations than with the significance of Jesus Christ (as the Son of God) for God's adoption of all persons. Access to this adoption occurs through faith.

The letter to the Ephesians, which was written by someone close to Paul, produces in 2:10 the unique formulation: "we are . . . created in Christ Jesus for good works, which God prepared beforehand, that we should walk in them." Accordingly, the works that Christians (should) do are like clothes that God has already made and that they must only put on. One already knew from Qumran texts (hymns) that "all works of righteousness are in God"; but that meant nothing other than that God engages only in works of righteousness. The passage from Ephesians becomes clearer, however, in one of the new texts (4Q 215, 7f.) where we read: "For he prepared their deeds before they [i.e., the doers] were created, and measured out their portion from service to righteousness." Here the deeds of the righteous truly are created beforehand. (Regarding "measuring out," see 2 Cor. 10:12ff. with the mention of "measure . . . by.")

Conclusion: Hope for God's mercy and the problem of righteousness were important topics in Judaism of that time. This is particularly reflected in the texts from Qumran. Because Paul attaches, in a radical way, all these motifs and ideas to Jesus Christ, he holds to a unique division of history into the unfortunate period before and the potentially joyful period after the coming of the Messiah. This aspect is absent in Qumran. The texts about the Messiah or the messiahs are not connected with such expectations.

Faith

In intertestamental Judaism "to believe" generally became the essence of the active relationship with the God of Israel. That is also fundamentally the case in Paul.

Paul repeatedly refers to Habakkuk 2:4 as the basis of his teaching from scripture: "the righteous shall live by his faith." In the Hebrew as in the Greek, "faith" could also mean "faithfulness" here.

The same passage is also quoted in the Habakkuk commentary from Qumran: "But the righteous shall live by his faith [faithfulness]." "Interpreted, this concerns all those who observe the Law in the House of Judah, whom God will deliver from the House of

Judgement because of their suffering and because of their faith in the Teacher of Righteousness" (1QpHab 8:1; Vermes, 287). "Faithfulness" ("faith") is expressed here as doing of the law as well as personal faithfulness to the teacher of righteousness. As in the previously mentioned passage, the predicate "righteous" comes first. That means that the righteous person lives thus; this is his characteristic. How he became a righteous person is not the issue here. He only proves himself as such.

Conclusion: Habakkuk 2:4 is not only quoted in Paul [Rom. 1:17; Gal. 3:11] but also in Qumran. In Paul, becoming righteous stands in the foreground ("the righteous will live by faith"), whereas in Qumran the concern is with the means by which the faithfulness of faith is demonstrated. Paul stresses the starting point, the Qumran text the lasting evidence of faith. Thus, the two could supplement each other and form contrasts that are not mutually exclusive.

Chapter 9

The End of the World
and the New Jerusalem

We have already discussed the messianic expectations in the
Qumran texts. Here the issue is the end of the world itself and, in
particular, the problem of whether in individual documents from
Qumran there is an expectation that the end is imminent.

The anticipation of the end time (eschatology) reflected in individual documents from Qumran is not uniform. The judgment that
"the community" of Qumran saw itself as the community of the
last generation and that the coming of God or of the Messiah was
imminent is misleading.

Rather, the following is correct: In many documents from
Qumran a great interest in the end time is found, and there is also
a series of depictions of the "heavenly Jerusalem" that are quite
similar to the portrayal in Revelation 21. But all of that is to be
sharply distinguished from the view that one's own generation is
that in which the Messiah is coming.

In the commentary on Habakkuk it is expressly stated that "the
final age shall be prolonged, and shall exceed all that the Prophets
have said; for the mysteries of God are astounding" (1QpHab 7:7f.;
Vermes, 286). To be sure, the prophet Habakkuk is interpreted
and actualized in stages in this commentary, but that does not
mean that the interpreter worked here from the schema of prophetic promise and fulfillment in the end time.

Furthermore, there is in the Qumran texts the phrase "at the
end of days," which sometimes refers to present powers, as in the
commentaries on Isaiah, Hosea, and Habakkuk as well as in the
collection of passages interpreted in 4QFlorilegium. In the commentary on Habakkuk, for example, the phrase refers to the oppo-

nents of the covenant. But we have already seen that, according to this document, the actual end itself is prolonged.

Only in the *Damascus Rule* (CD 4:4; Vermes, 85) is there mention made that the sons of Zadok, the chosen ones, "shall stand at the end of days." But according to CD 6:11 (Vermes, 87) the teacher of righteousness was already "at the end of days," that is, in the past. Therefore, one could even ask whether the phrase "at the end of days" is to be understood at all in terms of the end time and whether it does not simply mean "now, in the last days," much as someone today might refer to "last week," without thereby thinking of the end of the world.

Conclusion: Several Qumran documents speak of the "end of days," but it is not clear whether this really means that the end of the world stands directly ahead.

Only in the newly available document 4Q 385 is there an imminent expectation for the future: "the days will quickly rush by until all humanity will say: Do not the days hasten when Israel will receive its land? . . . I want to measure the time and shorten the days and the years a little."

Just as in 2 Thessalonians 2:6–7 there is something or someone that "restrains" the revealing of the evil one, so in 1Q 27 (*Book of Mysteries*) there are people who "restrain the wonderful mysteries." In 2 Thessalonians, however, the negative is stopped, while in 1Q 27 it is the coming of the positive that is restrained. In both texts the "restrainers" are concrete but obscure powers that block the anticipated coming of the next phase. The view of history that is presupposed, however, is common even in the details of the language.

The Qumran texts discuss the kingdom of God only in the sense of the sovereignty exercised by God already now in heaven (princely household) or over the righteous (thus 4Q 286 mentions one who "bears God's kingdom in the midst of the peoples"). Humanity is able to align itself in the heavenly princely household by means of purity and hymnic prayers. But in 1QM 6:5f., God's future kingdom is mentioned in terms of military supremacy ("a shield and a sword, to bring down the slain by the judgement of God. . . . And sovereignty shall be to the God of Israel, and he shall accomplish mighty deeds by the saints of his people" [Vermes, 111]). Here we probably have an interpretation of Daniel 7:14–18 to which the connection between "saints" and "kingdom" ("sovereignty") refers: The interpretation of the same passage is somewhat different if the kingdom occurs with the end of Israel (4Q 252 5:3).

No mention is ever made of a coming or a future revelation of the kingdom of God, not even of an entry of persons into the kingdom of heaven. Parables of the kingdom of God are not found in the Qumran texts. Thus, there are significant differences from Jesus' proclamation.

Conclusion: There is for the Qumran texts no immediate, imminent expectation of the end. That is consistent with there also being no references at all to the advent of the Messiah. The Qumran texts almost always speak of the kingdom of God differently from the way Jesus does.

Conclusion
What Do the Qumran Texts Offer That Is New?

The Character of the Qumran Texts

The texts that were found in the caves of Qumran do not form a uniform "work." Nor are they an expression of a uniform theology or even a simply linear theological development. The collection includes documents of quite varied contents. Aside from the texts treated here, also found in the caves were fragments of almost every biblical book and many fragments of the remaining intertestamental literature. All the texts are instructive, particularly for the religious (but also for the political) life of the first century B.C.E.

Traces of early Christianity cannot be found. But in many respects, that to which these texts attest comes closer to early Christianity than anything else in Judaism. This is true of perspectives of faith as well as practice.

What Is Lacking in Qumran?

The most important absence is that there is no notion of the kingdom of God that would be comparable to Jesus' conception; there is no kingdom of God that is coming or that is to be disclosed; there is only a present one in heaven, or one in which those engaged in hymnic prayers participate or whose bearer among the nations is Israel. Only in one passage, in a military interpretation, can one find a reference to Daniel 7.

Because of these differences there are also no parables of the kingdom of God. Absent also is any reference to our understanding of time, which we find in Paul, namely, that the decisive redemption has already occurred and that everything in the future is only a consequence of it.

There is lacking the high degree of attention to individuals found in early Christian documents, which in general are oriented toward particular charismatics (Jesus, Paul, Peter, John) and which also express this in biographical genres. Even the notes about Enoch and Noah in the Qumran texts are far from biographies if one omits the stories of Noah's birth.

The absence of these elements indicates that besides the kingdom-of-God eschatology, the second fundamental pillar of primitive Christianity is also absent in the Qumran texts: an emphasis on charismatic gifts of the Spirit.

Thus, miracle stories and exorcisms are also absent. The miracles of Isaiah 35 and 61 are only expected in the future. Only in the later narrative of the accounts about Abraham (1QapGen 20:28–29) do we find healing and exorcism by laying on of hands. There Abraham says to Pharaoh: "And I prayed for him to be healed and laid my hands on his head, and the plague was removed from him and the evil spirit was driven from him, and he was restored." Magical texts are certainly found among the new texts (4Q 560: against evil spirits), but there are no stories of success.

Only in a single new document (4Q 477) are evildoers mentioned by name in Qumran. The "teacher of righteousness" is nameless—comparable in the New Testament only to the nameless "disciple whom Jesus loved." In contrast, from the early period of Christianity an abundance of names are known to us in concrete instances. This different "style" is not superficial but is above all an indication of gifts of the Spirit in early Christianity. Thus also lacking are exhortations or arguments based directly on a particular community. The letter genre is used only rarely. Nevertheless, a commonality with early Christian letters can be seen in that brotherly love (vis-à-vis companions in the group) is mentioned more often than love of neighbor (vis-à-vis human beings in general).

Naturally, there is no mention in Qumran of martyrdoms, accounts of martyrs, or even sacrificial deaths. Only certain categories of thought are "placed at one's disposal," such as the association between atonement and ransom (*Temple Scroll,* col. 63: "Accept expiation for thy people Israel whom thou hast redeemed" [Vermes, 155]).

There is also no mention of a general resurrection of the dead. Whether 4Q 521 speaks of a general resurrection or of specific miracles remains an open question ("Then he will heal the sick, raise the dead").

The Most Significant Points of Contact with the New Testament

The Qumran texts provide the genres of exhortation, catalogs of virtues and vices, accounts of visions, midrashes (running commentaries on scripture), descriptions of the heavenly Jerusalem, and above all, apocalypses of history.

From a theological perspective, mediating figures between God and humanity are important (angel, devil, Messiah); images of the end of time are sketched.

However, the truly significant commonalities are found in two areas: Early Christianity exhibited clear similarities with several Qumran texts where it was understood as a conversion movement within Israel for its renewal. Hence the large areas of agreement in the conceptions of conversion and baptism, dualism ("children of light") and the panel of twelve, wilderness and encampment as the place of renewal, the new covenant, those who are "called," and persons of the divine goodwill. And for such a renewal community of the perfected, procedures for exclusion of the unworthy also had to be considered.

The second area of agreement has to do particularly with Pauline theology, especially Paul's statements regarding sin and grace, right up to the justification of the ungodly (1QH 4:29–31; 7:16–18). The analogies in the Qumran texts are mostly found in hymns, for this genre is otherwise also the place of the most profound piety in the Judaism of this period.

The two themes of gracious election and calling, in which one finds the greatest similarities to the Qumran texts, are also presented in such a way that they are bound together.

Concluding Observations

Certainly in this book we have given up the claim to all the ingredients of a spy thriller. Nevertheless we have hit upon a very exciting story, for we were able to follow the initial stages of the path in which Christianity grew out of Judaism. Because we took a more cautious way than is normally taken, we have freed the Qumran texts from their artificial isolation of being treated as texts of a mere sect. We have been under the impression that one had been too strongly immunized against the texts because of their classification as sect writings, and they had thus been mummified. In reality, however, these commentaries and prayers, hymns and apocalypses are at the heart of the Judaism of the time of Jesus.

Jesus emerged out of Judaism of this kind. The texts show us a piety that expects that by rigorous fulfillment of the will of God and by precise observance of the calendar and of all Temple rules the world can still be rightly ordered; that reality will still accommodate itself to God's name if only perfect righteousness would be practiced somewhere. Good and evil, reward and punishment are then wonderfully and suggestively distributed. This fantastic relationship to reality is a prelude to the still somewhat more daring statements of early Christianity that Jesus the Messiah could raise the dead with a simple word; indeed, that he himself is the Word by which the world came into being. For now it is no longer a whole group of observant righteous persons on whom everything depends—there is only one single righteous person and the entire, incomprehensible company of all salvation is in him.

Index of References

Talmud

b.Yoma
84b   68

Classical

Pliny
Natural History
5:73   31